JESUS CULTURE

JESUS CULTURE

LIVING A LIFE THAT TRANSFORMS THE WORLD

BANNING LIEBSCHER

DESTINY IMAGE® PUBLISHERS, INC.

P.O. Box 310, Shippensburg, PA 17257-0310

"Speaking to the Purposes of God for This Generation and for the Generations to Come."

This book and all other Destiny Image, Revival Press, MercyPlace, Fresh Bread, Destiny Image Fiction, and Treasure House books are available at Christian bookstores and distributors worldwide.

For a U.S. bookstore nearest you, call 1-800-722-6774.
For more information on foreign distributors, call 717-532-3040.
Reach us on the Internet: www.destinyimage.com.

ISBN 10: 0-7684-3100-X
ISBN 13: 978-0-7684-3100-1

For Worldwide Distribution, Printed in the U.S.A.

3 4 5 6 7 8 9 10 11 / 13 12 11 10

DEDICATION

I dedicate this book to SeaJay

"I know your name"

ACKNOWLEDGMENTS

SeaJay, I'm the most blessed man alive. God was good to me when He brought you into my life. Thanks for all your support and sacrifice and for believing in my dreams. You truly are amazing and the love of my life.

Mom and Dad, thanks for always being my biggest fans, loving me, and speaking identity into me.

My three beautiful kids, Ellianna, Raya, and Lake, I could not have written this book without your support. Let's change the world together.

Brandy, thanks for getting enough education for both of us. You are a great sister.

Bill, thanks for allowing me to stand on your shoulders. Your life has been the greatest message I have ever heard. Thanks for taking a chance on a young man.

Kris, thanks for coming alongside me and believing in me. Your encouragement, wisdom, and friendship mean the world to me.

Danny, you are a gift from God. I shudder to think of where I would be without you in my life. I am forever grateful for all that you have done for me and my family.

Dann, what do I say? I am your Padawan. Thanks for being my best mentor, professor, and friend. Thanks also for letting me interrupt your life over the last 13 years.

Lou, you are my Martin Luther King Jr. I thank God for linking our hearts together. You have placed courage inside of me and your life inspires me in ways you may never know. Thanks for showing me why I'm alive.

Cindy, the Mama of Revivalists, your encouragement, support, and example are massive in my life. Thanks for pouring into me.

Allison, thank you for being patient with this first-time author. Words cannot express how grateful I am for your help in getting this book ready. I pray all of your dreams come true.

A.J., thanks for making me look like a genius. Your help was inestimable, effulgent, and resplendent.

Carol, thanks not only for your help with the book but also your encouraging words. This "words of affirmation" guy appreciates it.

Pam, you have been such an encouragement for me to write. Over the past few years your voice has inspired me to keep going and keep believing that I can do it. Thank you for the help with the book, but beyond that thank you for encouraging me to write.

Darren, thanks for all of your research.

I have been blessed over the years with the greatest teams in the world: Jerry, Erica, Nathan, Kim, Chris, Melissa H., Brandon, Ben, and the rest of the current team, as well as Linda, Gabe, Melissa, Loni, Ken, and the rest of our past team. Thank you for all that you do and have done. My dreams are being fulfilled, and it is because of your sacrifice and passion. I love working with you all.

Last but not least, this book has been formed over the last 13 years because of the lives of some of the most radical young revivalists I've ever encountered. All of those at Legacy, Awakening, and Jesus Culture—thanks for burning and being the message.

ENDORSEMENTS

God is raising up an army of young, on-fire revivalists destined to awaken the nations of the earth. *Jesus Culture* gives them their marching orders to set on fire a new generation of passionate change agents.

CINDY JACOBS
Co-founder and President, Generals International

Read this book and you'll be changed. Live this book and the world will changed too.

PETE GREIG
Co-founder—The 24/7 Prayer Movement
Director of Prayer—at Holy Trinity Church, Brompton, London
Facilitator—Campus America initiative

Jesus Culture is not just another book about revival. The pages cry out for change with the kind of urgency that makes you want to jump out of your chair and onto your knees. It rekindles a passion that I believe should be in the heart of every Christian who is intimately connected to Jesus and eager to see the world experience the life-changing power of the Savior. Pastor Banning brings all the essential elements of revival into balance: the importance of spiritual authority while allowing a burning love for Jesus to develop into a passion for prayer to not only see but demonstrate the supernatural. I would recommend this book for any young person or pastor alike, wanting to be reminded again of the cry of God's heart for cities saved and entire nations turned to Him.

JUDAH SMITH
Pastor—Generation Church, an exploding
youth ministry of The City Church, Seattle, WA

In a deteriorating world system of false foundation, there arises a God breed of modern-day John the Baptizers willingly and fully committed to Christ and His Kingdom culture no matter what! Banning Liebscher is one such champion leader in the emerging youth generation, crying out to the generations of the nations and preparing the way of the Lord. This is a must-read prophetic and instructional manual to inform and equip you for what is ahead.

DR. CHÉ AHN
Senior Pastor—Harvest Rock Church, Pasadena, CA
President—Harvest International Ministry

God always provides a prophetic voice for each generation to mobilize and equip them for their destiny. Banning Liebscher is one of those voices for this generation. Few have the privilege to experience a sustained move of God that transforms communities such as Redding, California. Jesus Culture contains real, life-changing experiences and lessons that will both inspire and equip those who feel the call as a new-breed revivalist. I highly recommend that anyone who hungers for a move of God devour this book.

RICHARD CRISCO
Senior Pastor—Rochester First Assembly of God,
Rochester, Mi
Former Pastor of Student Ministries—
Brownsville Assembly of God, Pensacola, Fl

This book gives a generation permission to live a powerful life with God. It shows you that there is freedom to pursue your passions and impact the culture around you for the Kingdom. There is revelation in this book that will go into your foundation and accelerate you into your destiny. But underlying all of it, it inspires you to pursue intimacy with Him.

KELLY CLARK
Professional half-pipe snowboarder
Winter Olympic Gold Medalist,
and winner of two Winter X Games Gold Medals

Above the incessant noise of human activity
we have "heard the sound of marching"
that tells us God is on the move.

—ARTHUR WALLIS[1]

It is God revealing Himself to man
in awful holiness and irresistible power.
It is such a manifest working of God
that human personalities are overshadowed,
and human programs abandoned.
It is man retiring into the background
because God has taken the field.
It is the Lord making bare His holy arm,
and working in extraordinary power
on saint and sinner.

—ARTHUR WALLIS[2]

TABLE OF CONTENTS

SECTION IV THOSE WHO PRAY

SECTION V HEALING REVIVALISTS

FOREWORD BY BILL JOHNSON

One of my greatest joys is to help others find their purpose in life. I wish I could say it happens often; it doesn't. But when it does, it is so wonderful that I actually end with up a greater sense of personal completeness. We are all strengthened when someone we care about succeeds. Such is the case in my personal involvement with Banning Liebscher. He has said such an absolute "yes" to God, and he has stepped into the wonderful discovery of his calling much earlier in life than most and with a depth that is rare in people twice his age. And we are stronger because of it.

I did something a bit unusual for me while reading this book. I tried to remove myself and my knowledge of Banning from the picture as much as possible. I then pondered over the material as though it were the writings of a highly respected revivalist in their 70s, still burning for God. I was amazed. It still fit. It was then I knew that what I felt about this book was more than a personal bias. The maturity and depth of Banning's ministry is well represented in *Jesus Culture*. This book will cross generational lines, as it should, and bring marching orders for a people hungry for eternal significance.

What you're about to read is amazingly refreshing. If it only contained the zealous declarations of what we ought to be doing, I'd still promote it. But it is so much more than that. This book comes from someone who speaks with a fresh fire from Heaven, laced with the wisdom gained through God's "crash course" in discovering His heart for the nations. And all of that comes from a life given to intimacy with God. Take a good look at *Jesus Culture*. It is a rare moment in life to read something with this potential for impact. Banning has captured the heart of a movement among the young that is spreading from nation to nation. They are sold-out lovers of God who are living offerings for the glory of God. The future of the Church never looked brighter.

BILL JOHNSON
Senior Pastor—Bethel Church
Redding, CA
Author—*When Heaven Invades Earth*
and *Face to Face With God*

FOREWORD BY LOU ENGLE

As I survey the chilled landscape of compromised religion in America, my attention is captured by a burning and shining lamp lighting up the skies over Northern California. There, in the otherwise very normal town of Redding, a sign and a wonder is taking place at a church called Bethel.

Spiritual sons and daughters raised in a house dedicated to the Father are running out from the conspicuous Presence in their church building and carrying Him into the streets. Miracles are occurring, healings are taking place, a town is being transformed, and thousands are going out to see this burning and shining lamp at Bethel. But Bethel is more than a lamp. It is a breeding ground for young revivalists, preachers, and prophets who are being defined by God's dreams, fueled by fasting and prayer, and armed with revelation and supernatural faith. Together they are a voice among many others, passionately contending for breakthrough in the Kingdom of God. With groups of people beginning to burn like this, maybe we'll see real "global warming" that will heat up the planet with the fires of revival.

My friend and comrade for years, Banning Liebscher, is at the burning center of this youth movement. Though a young man he has been a powerful spiritual encouragement to me for many years. Often he has kindled my prophetic faith for the future. In him I see a forerunner of a great army of revival.

I believe his vision set forth in this book will light the candles in the hearts of young men and women all around the world and set off an explosion of faith for the appearance in power of our supernatural God.

Defined by Dreams

In his book *Engaging the Powers,* Walter Wink describes a phenomenon that is applicable to this generation:

Consciously or unconsciously, one lives not only one's life, but the life of one's time.... Are our dreams, for example, to some degree facets of a larger mass dream that is beginning to happen in the world?...To put it another way, when God wants to initiate a new movement in history, God does not intervene directly, but sends us dreams and visions that can, if attended to, initiate a process.[1]

Forty years ago, one man gave voice to a dream that resonated in the hearts of a generation defined by dreams of freedom. That man, Martin Luther King Jr., mobilized a movement among an oppressed and marginalized people that shook the pillars of injustice and cut off the chains of segregation. It was a revolution that changed the face of a nation and transformed a generation in America.

Once again, a young dreamer generation is rising, and their dreams are from Heaven. Once again, God, the greatest countercultural Dreamer, is commissioning them to release the roar: *I have a dream and let my people go.*

I have a dream! Let my people go! Challenge the worldwide epidemic slave trade. I have a dream! Let my people go! Give us the orphaned, broken children of this collapsing secular civilization. I have a dream! Let my people go! Give us the greatest healing and salvation revival in history. Dreams were meant to come true. "Would the God of love fasten your soul to a dead-end dream?"[2]

Fueled by Fasting

The emerging generation of revivalists is hungry for revelation; their hunger is fueled by the discipline of fasting. As Walter Wink writes in his book, *Engaging the Powers:* "The slack decadence of culture-Christianity cannot produce athletes of the spirit. Those who are the bearers of tomorrow undergo what others might call disciplines...to stay spiritually alive."[3]

A young university student had been on a Daniel fast—fasting meats and sweets—for two years, praying for the end of abortion in America. After the election of George Bush in 2004, clearly a pro-life president, the young man asked God for permission to eat normally again. He determined that if God did not give him a confirmation to continue the fast, he would break it the following day.

That evening, just before midnight, my young intercessor joined one of his friends to study. Seeing an unfamiliar student, he introduced himself. The stranger replied, "Hello, my name is Daniel Fast." He was a Jewish kid.

My young friend knew this was the confirmation he was praying for, and so he continued his Daniel fast. God seemed to be shouting to him, "Oh Daniel, you are highly esteemed in Heaven!"

Many other young people across the nation are entering into fasting lifestyles. They are becoming burning and shining lamps ablaze for the jealousy of God. They are clearing the decks and making their lives a landing strip for revelation. And like Daniel, they are being rewarded with dreams, words of knowledge, and supernatural power. I believe they are a prototype of this end-time generation. Prophets are forged in the deserts of fasting, not the deserts of feasting.

Prevailing in Prayer

The last thing Jesus did before He left the earth was hold a prayer meeting. That prayer meeting opened Heaven and the tongue of fire exploded from the mouths of the newly-ordained New Testament revivalists. God will not change His methods. *"My house shall be called a house of prayer,"* is the roar of the Lord being heard across the earth (see Matt. 21:13). A phenomenon is taking place! Hundreds of millions of people in almost every nation pray on the same day, the Global Day of Prayer. "TheCall" has gathered hundreds of thousands world-wide in solemn assemblies of fasting and prayer.

A movement of 24/7 prayer is gaining momentum around the world. Ministries have sprung up to spearhead the movement, and young people are involved at ground level, playing a significant role in such efforts as the International House of Prayer (IHOP), Boiler Rooms, 48HOPs, 24/7 prayer, and now Justice House of Prayer (JHOP). All of them sponsor prayer initiatives in various countries. I believe the houses of prayer fueled by the young are just the beginning of what is to come.

Clearly the Lord is raising up a prayer standard to challenge the darkened, decadent soul of the age. A culture of prayer is what is needed, not a prayer meeting. The Muslims have a prayer culture but the Christian church has a prayer meeting. How will a nice little prayer meeting contend with the Muslim prayer culture? A great shift is occurring, and as it does, the tongue of fire and the move of miracles will turn the masses to Jesus and the cry will be heard once again, "What must we do to be saved?"

In 2000, before TheCall D.C. where 400,000 people gathered to pray and fast for our nation, I heard the audible voice of God in a night encounter. The voice rumbled through my soul, "America is receiving her apostles, prophets, and evangelists, but she has not yet seen her nazarites." Something is coming to America that has never been seen before; voices of truth and holiness like the nazarite, John the Baptist, will shake cities. The spirit and the power of Elijah will raise a dead generation. A special mission demands a special consecration.

Young men, young women, read this book and burn! Dare to dream the dreams of God. Prepare yourself to be a voice in the fires of fasting and prayer and then obey the spirit and be carried by the wind into a life of miracles, prophesy, and persecution.

LOU ENGLE
Founder of TheCall

SECTION I

THE NEW BREED OF REVIVALIST

THIS IS INARGUABLY the greatest hour in history, and you are invited to participate in the most monumental move of God the world has ever seen! The Lord wants the hearts of people across the earth, and He is awakening His Church to His desire.

I dream of entire cities and nations being saturated and transformed by the Presence of God—and I am devoted to seeing an army of healing revivalists raised up who demonstrate the Kingdom of God by releasing signs, wonders, and miracles. The Lord is restoring the supernatural to His Church through regular believers—just like you and me!

To undergird this activation, God is installing an entirely new mindset in us—a mentality founded upon the truth that *nothing is impossible*. In order to move in the authority given to us, this new breed of revivalists needs to rearrange certain perceptions in order to operate in all that is available to us through the Cross. This renewed attitude is founded upon the awareness that *if God is with us, then who can be against us!?*

You, my friend, have been set up for success! Your life is crucial to the plans of God. The dreams ingrained in your heart are resident there because God wants to use you to bring revival in your particular realm of society. The passions of your heart are significant and intimately linked to His longing and commissioning for nations to be discipled and impacted for Him!

JESUS CULTURE

CHAPTER 1

THE GREATEST HOUR OF HISTORY

Let me get straight to the point. I believe you are reading this book because you are one of a new breed of revivalist emerging in the earth. God has chosen you to be an integral part of His plan for worldwide revival. His heart is longing for the nations to turn to Him, and in the midst of deep darkness and despair He is pouring out His Spirit. The Lord's glory is rising on His people and shining bright in cities and nations around the world.

This outpouring is why *you* are alive, and nothing else will satisfy. You hold this book in your hand because you were created to take cities and disciple nations. You have been called to participate in the most monumental move of God in history!

Acts 17 says:

> From one man He made every nation of men, that they should inhabit the whole earth; **and He determined the times set for them and the exact places where they should live**. God did this so that men would seek Him and perhaps reach out for Him and find Him, though He is not far from each one of us (Acts 17:26-27 NIV).

Do you know what that means? God searched throughout the corridors of eternity and decided to strategically place *you* in this exact dispensation of time. You could have been born hundreds of years ago, but you weren't—you were born in *this* very hour. You should jump out of bed every morning with a smile on your face and a bounce in your step because God has chosen to put you right here, right now, for the greatest *outpouring* the world has ever seen!

In 1999, Wesley Campbell visited Bethel Church and began to open my eyes to understand the hour in which we are living. During one of his messages, he quoted several statistics that completely floored me:

- The world's population didn't reach one billion until 1804.
- In 1960, 156 years later, that number tripled to three billion people.
- In 1999, 39 years after that, the world's population doubled to six billion people.
- Shortly, there will be more people alive on the earth than the total number of all who have ever lived.[1]

Clearly, we live in a time of off-the-charts acceleration. Along with the world's exploding population, the work of God is increasing with exponential growth. Wesley also shared the following statistics of the global Christian population:

- One third of everyone who has come to Christ since He ascended has done so in the last ten years (current as of 1999).
- Each week, one million people accept Jesus as their Lord and Savior.
- With the population propulsion and rate of salvations, there will shortly be more people

alive who confess Jesus as Lord than everyone in
history who has been saved and is in Heaven.[2]

Here's another statistic quoted recently by Bobby Conner: "It is
estimated that over the last decade, an average of 1,200 people have
become Christians in China every hour!"[3] Beyond massive numbers of
salvations, there are many other signs that point to the greatness of
what God is doing. Technological advances have made it possible to
spread the Gospel in ways we never imagined. The global prayer movement is stronger than ever before, blazing through the earth in prayer
closets, prayer rooms, living rooms, 24/7 houses of prayer, churches,
and stadiums. Continuous, fervent prayer is rumbling throughout the
nations and rising toward Heaven for worldwide revival.

The supernatural is being restored once again to the Church.
Signs, wonders, healings, and prophecy are becoming consistently
demonstrated—not just in crusades, but in everyday life both inside
and outside the church walls. And it's not only happening through
the hands of those in professional ministry. Soccer moms, business
people, teachers, children, and many others are witnessing the Word
being made manifest in their regular lives. For years, we primarily
heard these kinds of testimonies from missionaries and we rejoiced
with them. But now the supernatural is not prevalent only in third
world countries—the full Gospel of the Kingdom is being preached
with signs and wonders in the western nations.

If the worldwide awakening and Kingdom increase happening
right now were to end today, it would still go down in the history
books as the most extensive and accelerative revival of all time. Yet
what is absolutely thrilling is that we are only at the beginning stages
of what God purposes to do! He is intent on giving His Son what He
asked for: the nations of the earth as His inheritance (see Ps. 2:8). A
billion-soul harvest in the coming days has been prophesied. God is
setting us up for something extraordinarily big.

What a great day to be alive! We truly live in the greatest hour of
history. Every day I have an overwhelming sense of gratefulness for

what God is doing in the earth and that I am alive to be a part of it. This gratitude has fueled my passion to write *Jesus Culture,* because I believe it is one way I can fulfill the role God has given me. My role is to call out and raise up this new breed of revivalist—the burning ones who will listen to their Father's heartbeat and respond to His desire for cities and nations.

HEALING REVIVALISTS

Any time God wants to reveal Himself in a region, whether locally or nationally, to save the lost and transform society through His presence and power, He anoints individuals we call revivalists. The Book of Jonah powerfully illustrates this principle. Nineveh was a city lost in sin, but God's heart yearned for her and her people. In the midst of their depravity, He proceeded to invade their lives with grace and love. His first step in this plan was to visit a man named Jonah.

When God called Jonah, He released to him the authority and power necessary to see revival in Nineveh. Jonah became God's answer for that city. And God still works this way. His heart is aching to see entire cities turn to Him, so He is anointing revivalists like you and me who will carry His presence and power into families, villages, cities, regions, and nations.

There is a courage rising in this new breed that will change nations. The veteran youth minister and author Winkie Pratney says, "When God finds someone with the courage to preach, pray, and live a life before Him of holiness and compassion, He can literally change the face of a nation."[4]

Jonah 1:1 says, *"Now the word of the Lord came to Jonah."* The word of the Lord is coming to men and women and their hearts are awakening toward God. They are overwhelmed with a passion to see revival and are no longer satisfied with simply attending church. They are unfulfilled by living a life that doesn't shape world history. They have been captured by the promise of a Spirit-led renaissance, and their hearts are attentive to what God is resolute to accomplish. Arthur Wallis, a leader in the charismatic movement in the United

Kingdom, identified this awakening with the birth of revival in his book, *In the Day of Thy Power*:

> Revival involves two awakening cries: God crying to man, *"Awake, awake...O Zion"* (Is. 52:1), and man crying to God, *"Awake, awake, put on strength, O arm of the Lord; awake as in the days of old"* (Is. 51:9 NASB). When the voice of the Lord has awakened the church, the voice of the church will awaken the Lord, and the power of God will be manifested in the saving of sinners. When it has seemed that for a long time the Almighty has slumbered, the cry of the church pierces the Heavens, *"Let God arise, let His enemies be scattered..."* (Ps. 68:1).[5]

The word of the Lord is once again invigorating revivalists who have an all-consuming longing for the glory of the Lord to cover the earth, and they will not be deterred. Years ago I heard a quote—which I believe was from Mario Murillo—that connects the importance of a people who refuse to be deterred with revival: "Ninety percent of revival is getting to a place where unshakeable resolve is born."

Every year the Bethel School of Supernatural Ministry brims with hundreds of new students from around the world who have come to be trained because of their desire to change the world. Many of them have sold everything or left their homes and families because they know their lives were meant to guide the course of history. They represent millions around the world whose impassioned cries for the presence of God are being released, and I see the Lord responding by anointing people with authority and power. Through these encounters, they are realizing that their destiny is intimately connected to revival, and they are surrendering with joyful obedience as the Lord sends them out.

God is reviving His Church because He wants cities and nations. I dream of entire cities being saturated in the presence of God, knowing the truth of the Gospel, and personally encountering His love and power. My devotion is to see the Church demonstrating the Kingdom of God by engaging people with the raw power and radical love of God. This is what possesses me, and this is the army I am called to raise up.

MY STORY

Though I grew up in a Christian environment, I had never even heard of revival until I was 19. I was from a solid Christian home, attended a conservative Baptist church, and went to a Christian school. I clearly remember, when I was four, sitting on my mom's lap on our old leather couch in the living room and accepting Jesus as my Savior. Then, at 17, I encountered God in a powerful way at Bethel Church in Redding, California. Kneeling by the steps at the front of the sanctuary, I surrendered my life completely to God and went home that night knowing I was called to preach the Gospel.

From that moment on I began to vigorously pursue God, and my life was consumed with love for Jesus. Ray Larson was the senior pastor and Scott Anderson was the youth pastor. I was blessed to have such great men pour into my life as a teenager. They called out the destiny that was on my life and inspired me to pursue all that God had for me. After I made the decision to pursue God with all of my heart, I lost all my friends. It wasn't even a conscious choice I made; I simply was headed in a different direction. My new focus in life made it impossible to continue doing the same things I had always done. My friends hadn't made the same choice I had; therefore, our paths separated. I was grieved over losing my friends, but I determined in my heart to follow Jesus. He was faithful and brought new friends around me. I began to devour the Word of God, listen to sermons, and read books that fueled this new flame.

When I was 19, I started a youth internship at Bethel Church. A few months after I started interning, Bill Johnson became our senior pastor. Before then, a handful of us at Bethel had been experiencing "renewal" at another church in town whose pastor had returned from the Toronto Airport Vineyard and had started holding weekly meetings. There I experienced the Lord in a way I'd never known. I stood on the prayer lines during the ministry times, weeping, overwhelmed by the presence of God. I remember walking into the services so happy that all I could do was smile and hug people. I didn't know it was the joy of the Lord because I didn't know there was such a thing; I just knew I loved being in those meetings where the presence of God was so strong.

Bill not only brought renewal to Bethel, he opened my eyes to the concept and history of worldwide revival. During that season, I consumed every book I could find about revival. It was so exciting to learn about the different outpourings of the Holy Spirit that had taken place in history. And it wasn't long before I realized that this is the reason I am alive. I was born to see His manifest presence coming to cities with millions being swept into the Kingdom of Heaven— entire cities and nations being transformed by the power of God. These were the things I began to daydream about, and this is what I knew I would spend the rest of my life pursuing. Desperate to find out what God could do through my life, I was gripped by the statement J.C. Pollock made to D.L. Moody, one of the great evangelists of the 19th century: "Moody, the world has yet to see what God will do with a man fully consecrated to Him."[6] I wanted to give myself fully to God for revival.

Bill also introduced me to men and women of the past whom God had anointed as revivalists—people like John Wesley, George Whitefield, Charles Finney, John Alexander Dowie, John G. Lake, Evan Roberts, William Seymour, Maria Woodworth Etter, William Branham, A.A. Allen, Aimee Semple McPherson, Oral Roberts, Kathryn Kuhlman, and John Wimber, to name just a few. I couldn't get enough of these revivalists. As I connected with their lives, I felt a new passion burning deep within me.

Then I found out that there were people alive who had a revival anointing. This was too much. The level of anointing I was reading about was still available today? After my encounter with God at 17, deep down inside I could feel my call to revival, but I was never able to put words to it. Now I was being introduced to a realm of God I previously didn't know existed. I was utterly wasted for revival, captivated with Jesus, and intoxicated with pursuing the nation's restoration to Him!

Then I met Lou Engle. He ministered at a Sunday night service a few years after Bill had come to Bethel. I had heard about him from some friends in Sacramento, California, who described him as a Christian drill sergeant with a voice made raspy by years of fervent prayer for revival. I sat in the front row, my heart burning as he preached. Lou spoke of prayer and revival, and it was as if I could hear God shouting to me through his ministry. He ended his message that night with a call for anyone who wanted to be an intercessor for revival to come forward. I rushed to the stage and lay on the steps with hundreds of other people. God sovereignly met me there and ignited a fire in me that has not stopped burning; in fact, it has increased. Lou imparted to me devoted earnestness for prayer and rapture for wholehearted consecration unto the Lord.

God used Bill and Lou to open the book of my life and show me why I'm alive. They drew back the curtains of prophetic potential and allowed me to see what God had for me and all that was possible for someone who would give himself completely for revival. Through them, the Lord reached deep inside me and awakened my destiny, fanning a blaze for the King and His Kingdom. I knew I was called to be a revivalist who walked in prayer and power to see cities taken and entire nations turn to God.

MY CALL

Soon after He called me to be an intercessor and revivalist, the Lord began to reveal another layer of His call for my life. By this time I was 23 and had already been a youth pastor for a few years. One night I had a dream that I was in the military. I was standing in the front row of a group of about 20 soldiers standing in formation down the middle of a suburban street. All the other soldiers were younger than I, and we were facing a drill sergeant who was showing us how to use our hands (which I believe represented prayer). All of a sudden, some of the soldiers began to run away from the formation into the homes in the neighborhood.

At first the drill sergeant didn't say anything, but when two young men at the back of our group took off running, he turned to me and another soldier and said, "Go get them." We pursued them down an alleyway that led to a dirt field where they got into a white car from the 1970s. As they sped off, I ran up alongside the car and grabbed onto the driver's side door. The window was down so I reached in and began to wrestle violently with the driver, trying to extract him out of the speeding car. Eventually I began to overcome him in the struggle, pulled him partway through the window, and finally succeeded in getting him out of the car. My companion accomplished the same with the other boy. We proudly walked these young soldiers back into formation, knowing our mission was accomplished. Through this dream and many subsequent dreams and prophetic words, the Lord called me to a fervent pursuit of a generation—to show them their purpose as revivalists.

THE PENNY AND 1948

In the summer of 2005, I started a prophetic journey that unveiled an even clearer picture of my call to raise up revivalists. I was scheduled to be the opening speaker at our annual Jesus Culture Conference in Redding and was unsure of what to share. I went to bed the night before the conference expecting the Lord to speak to me in a dream and bring clarity regarding my message.

God is always talking to us, and we must incline our ear to hear His voice. One of the most significant ways God speaks to me is through dreams. Over the years some of the most profound revelations or directions I've received from God have come in the night season. Throughout the Bible we see God communicating to people through dreams. But dreams are just one of the many different ways that God speaks to us. He also speaks through prophetic words, divine circumstances, His still small voice, and "coincidences" when our heart is tuned to the language of the Spirit. The written Word is the basis for our life, and every one of these methods God uses to speak to us must be congruent with the message of Scripture.

Sure enough, that night I had a dream in which I was calling people on the phone and asking, "How did the penny affect you in 1948?" When I woke up, I knew God was speaking to me. From my study of revival history, I understood 1948 had to do with the Healing Revival, and I felt that the penny was a play on the words "one sent" (like "one cent").

That day, I studied 1948 and quickly found out more about its significance in God's calendar. That year was an epic year in the Body of Christ. Not only did Israel once again become a nation, but also the Lord released an anointing in the Church that was staggering.[7] God dispensed power through men and women that ushered hundreds of thousands into the Kingdom and reignited the Church with fresh vision. Randy Bozarth, the former Vice President of Christ for the Nations, describes 1948 in his book, *The Voice of Healing*:

> Clearly by 1948 a new period on God's timetable had begun. It would be a period in which He would once again demonstrate His presence to the multitudes. He would lift the burden of sickness and pain by supernatural healings. He would encourage the faith of many by unusual signs and wonders.[8]

David Edwin Harrell writes about this time period that there was a "worldwide explosion of healing revivalism."[9] In my study I also encountered the exponential momentum of anointing the Lord had been releasing through many men and women. Although I don't have the time here to give an exhaustive study of each of these anointed revivalists, I do want to give a brief overview. And I encourage you to study these individuals in more depth, because their lives are extremely relevant for your journey as a revivalist. They reveal our inheritance and lineage and declare prophetically to us.

As I write about how I have studied and received from different men and women of God, I want to explain to you how I interact with their lives. Many of those I have great respect and honor for have not ended their lives well or have struggled with sin and made grievous mistakes. I believe we can and should celebrate the grace on the life of a man or woman of God without having to be blind to their short-comings or weaknesses. My life has been greatly impacted and influenced by a man who was an adulterer and murderer. I drink from the well of wisdom and understanding of a man who descended into promiscuity and immorality later in his life. Of course, I am talking about King David and his son, King Solomon. I do not believe that a person ending his or her life in a regrettable way means that person never had a heart for God. The sin in a human life does not negate the genuine revelation that person received or the ministry he or she moved in. If that were true, I would have to throw out the Book of Proverbs and most of the Psalms. I am a firm believer that we can "eat the meat and throw out the bones."

Some of the revivalists I mention in this book, as well as others I have received from, never experienced lasting victory over besetting sin. But I can still celebrate the grace on their lives and receive from them. The end of their lives does not cancel out their previous victories. I am, of course, grieved by the way some of them became isolated and unteachable. I am also grieved at how, in some instances, the Body of Christ abandoned these revivalists in their darkest hours. As you study the lives of both past and current revivalists, you will find many of them had glaring weaknesses and shortcomings. These too can be lessons about how to be successful when living as a revivalist. My heart for you is that you will be able to receive from these men and women of God and not have stolen from you what God wants to release to you through the grace on their lives.

In 1946 an angel visited William Branham, a poor Kentucky preacher, and told him he would take healing to the nations. The angel explained that he would display two signs that would give people faith to see the miraculous. Two years later, in 1948, Branham's ministry was drawing thousands of people with incredible impact and results. His ministry was marked by supernatural phenomena and miracles.

The first of the two signs in his ministry was an unusual ability to diagnose physical conditions, prefaced by a show of red bumps that appeared on his arm when he held the hand of a sick person. Witnesses observed that when these red bumps appeared on Branham's arm, he could identify any demonically induced sickness with 100 percent accuracy. When the blemishes disappeared, the person was healed. This happened thousands of times.

The other sign was a gift to see open visions over people. An orb of light would come into the room and hover over a certain individual. Many people witnessed this light and someone even took a photograph of it. When the light lingered over a person, Branham stopped everything and an open vision appeared in front of him. He then saw segments of the person's life play out in front of him like a movie. When he described what he saw, the person was healed or radically touched by the Spirit of God. Branham's ministry was known for raw power and supernatural activity, and hundreds of thousands were impacted by his faith. Many believe the anointing he walked in was the most powerful since the time of Jesus. [10]

Before 1948, Oral Roberts had been ministering healing for a season, but mainly in smaller venues. His healing ministry started in 1947, but in 1948 he established the Oral Roberts Evangelistic Association. His meetings began to gather multitudes of people hungry for healing or a fresh touch from God. He would sit in a chair on the stage as hundreds of people passed before him to receive healing prayer. Roberts was and is an incredible man of faith and vision and a powerful teacher of the Word. Through his ministry of meetings, books, television, and the university named after him, countless people have encountered God and received their breakthroughs in healing. [11]

In 1948 Billy Graham resigned his position with Youth for Christ and ventured out on his own and started the greatest individual evangelistic ministry in the world. The imprint that Graham has had on our world and the Church is undeniable. Millions are forever indebted to the faithfulness of this humble servant of God, whose principal desire was to bring the clear and simple message of Jesus to the world.[12]

In 1948 Kathryn Kuhlman held her first miracle service in Pittsburgh. Through these services, God would trumpet the message of healing to the world. Like Graham and Roberts, she had been preaching for years, but after a series of appointments with other ministers who delivered a message of healing, she began to bring the message that God still heals today. In 1947, she began to preach divine healing and was immediately impacted by the testimonies of people being healed in her meetings. This was the start of a long and incredibly powerful healing ministry that touched millions of people around the world. Her meetings were marked by the tangible manifestation of the presence of God. People would tell of being overwhelmed by the presence of God just when they walked into the building. Countless numbers were healed in her meetings just from being in the presence of the Lord.

Kuhlman was a woman who adored the Holy Spirit, and the Holy Spirit loved to hang out with her because she was a friend of God. She operated in the word of knowledge at a high level, and would know, through the Holy Spirit, certain ailments that were being healed during her meetings. She said things like, "Someone in the balcony to my left, someone in the balcony is being healed of back pain. You were in a car accident ten years ago and the doctors have given up on you. Right now you are being healed. Just receive your healing." Sure enough, someone was in the balcony who fit that exact description, and they were healed. She showed the Church more of what is available in our relationship with the Holy Spirit and influenced thousands of ministers, the most well-known being Benny Hinn.[13]

In 1947 Gordon Lindsay moved from Ashland, Oregon, where he was pastoring a local church, to head up William Branham's ministry. In 1948 Lindsay started a magazine called *The Voice of Healing* that spread accounts of the miracle-working power of God internationally. Eventually, *The Voice of Healing* grew into a movement that would connect around 50 healing revivalists who were ministering around the world and seeing incredible breakthrough in healing and salvations. Lindsay was a prolific writer who produced many books. Along with his wife, Freda, he started Christ for the Nations Institute in Dallas, Texas, which, to this day, is training revivalists to impact the nations of the earth.[14]

THE MESSAGE

Through my dream of the penny and 1948, the Lord began to speak to me about His intention to release the anointing that was present in 1948 once again. However, this time the message was that it was available to everyone. It wasn't going to rest just on a few individuals; it would be spread *en masse* across the Body of Christ. All those hungry enough would have access to the same level of anointing that Branham, Roberts, Graham, Kuhlman, and Lindsay moved in.

God never intended an anointing to remain on just one select individual. The promise that was initially fulfilled at Pentecost and will be ultimately fulfilled is that God *"will pour forth of* [His] *Spirit on **all mankind"*** (Acts 2:17 NASB). His desire and plan have always been to empower the entire Body of Christ to operate in that level of anointing. But He has specific strategies for fulfilling this plan. I have heard Bill Johnson describe it this way:

> God gives certain individuals a "spike" in human experience, not so they can merely gather people around themselves to minister to them, but that they would be positioned with favor to equip the saints, so that their "high point" becomes the new norm.

Thankfully, people throughout the Church are beginning to recognize and embrace the truth that every believer is eligible and, in fact, is called to walk in the anointing of the Holy Spirit. We are in a new season in the Body of Christ in which believers are no longer satisfied to sit back and watch platform ministers. They want to flow in that same anointing and see the world encounter God through them. It is the "day of the saints." There is a huge influx of ministries and churches that are changing how they do ministry in order to "[equip]... *the saints for the work of the ministry*" (Eph. 4:12). The penny in my dream was prophetic that I too was to have a part in raising up the saints and "sending" them.

A few months after I had the penny dream, I went to preach at the weekend services of a church in a suburb of Chicago. My wife and I flew in on Friday and went to dinner with the pastor and his family. While we were sitting around the table at the restaurant, our conversation turned to past moves of God in Chicago.

One cannot discuss revival in Chicago without talking about John Alexander Dowie. Dowie was a minister who lived in the area in the late 1800s and early 1900s. He had an incredible revelation of the healing power of God and is considered the main father of the current healing movement that began in the early 1900s. (John G. Lake was one prominent minister, among others, who was profoundly touched by his ministry.) Dowie established healing homes where the terminally ill came and stayed for weeks. They received prayer from people trained in healing ministry and were saturated in the truth found in Scripture concerning healing. The statistics of those healed from terminal illness in these homes are astounding. (Today, Cal Pierce is carrying on the same ministry through the Healing Rooms in Spokane, Washington.[15]) But Dowie's influence in Chicago went far beyond his healing ministry; he affected the entire city. Roberts Liardon, an author and expert on revival, in his book *God's Generals,* says it this way: "Never before or since has one man so captured a city. Dowie had great influence over the city of Chicago."[16]

In 1900 Dowie left Chicago and established a city called Zion, which is still there today. Since I was going to be in Chicago for a few days, I asked the pastor if we could visit Zion and spend some time praying there. That Sunday afternoon we drove to Zion, intending to take a tour of Dowie's home, Shiloh House. We arrived and went up to the door, expecting to meet the lady who was to give us the tour. When the pastor knocked on the door, the lights flickered in the house and all electric power went out in the region. No one came to the door, so we left and drove around the city for a while. We noticed that the power was out everywhere but didn't think much of it.

We returned to Dowie's house, and this time we got to go inside. It was an amazing experience to tour the house of such a giant of the faith. After an hour or so it was getting too dark to see well, but before we left the pastor sat down at a piano and we spent time worshiping and praying for the release of power in the nation again.

By that point, we sensed that the power outage was somehow prophetic, but we could not figure out what God was saying. I turned to one of the guys and said, "I think the power outage is prophetic, but it's bad if it means the power is going out, right? We don't want power to go *out* in the nation; we want it to be *on*."

As we were preparing to leave, one of the guys turned to me and asked, "Wouldn't it be crazy if the power came back on when we left?"

We agreed it would be a bit strange, then walked down the long hallway to the back door. The instant the door opened, all of the power was restored in the region. That was just too much! We stood there astonished, trying to comprehend what the Lord was telling us.

Then I got it. I turned to our group and said, "I understand what this means. Power has been lost, but it is being restored as we go out." That was it. That was what the Lord was telling us, and it was significant because we were in Dowie's house. Dowie made an impression on the city of Chicago like no other person. He influenced every area of society. Politics, business, religion, and education were all affected by the anointing on Dowie. Chicago, I believe, was on its way to becoming the first city in America that was completely saved. Liardon wrote about the impact Dowie had: "Soon there was scarcely a person in Chicago who had not heard the Gospel message."[17] But it stopped when Dowie left Chicago and planted a Christian community.

Please hear my heart, as I do not want to dishonor Dowie here. I believe the Church owes him more than most will ever know. I'm not trying to write an opinion on whether or not Dowie should have left Chicago, but I *am* saying that the influence and revelation of the power of God that had been impacting Chicago left when Dowie departed. In essence, when he moved inside a Christian community, he stopped extending out to impact the city. My point is that I believe the revelation of power that God had given to Dowie would have eventually transformed the city of Chicago.

God was speaking to me loud and clear: "I am restoring power to the Church again, to take cities when they go out." God is anointing individuals with power to impact cities and turn nations to God. But these people must be sent. They must, as Isaiah prophesied, *"Arise, shine"* (Isa. 60:1). This is my mandate—to raise up a generation upon whom the glory of the Lord has risen and to whom the nations will come.

I want to tell you about one more significant prophetic encounter. A few months after my experience at Dowie's house, one of our pastors at Bethel, Kevin Dedmon, had an encounter involving a man named Lonnie Frisbee. Lonnie Frisbee was a young hippie who had been saved in San Francisco and had become one of the catalysts for the Jesus Movement of the late sixties and early seventies. He was a primary reason for the explosive growth of both the Calvary Chapel and the Vineyard movements. Frisbee had a strong prophetic anointing, and the manifest presence of God was a distinctive mark of his ministry. Many people testified of signs and wonders happening in his meetings.

Before Kevin Dedmon joined the staff at Bethel, he was a Vineyard pastor in Southern California. Kevin knew Lonnie Frisbee and ministered to him before he died in 1993, but he did not understand the concepts of anointings, mantles, or inheritances at that point, so he never asked Frisbee to pray for him. When Kevin began to learn about past revivalists and the anointing they carried, he started to study the life of Frisbee. He found out that many years ago Frisbee had partnered with four other radical new Christians to start a Christian commune called the House of Acts in Novato, California. It just so happened that a month after this discovery in February 2006, Kevin was scheduled to minister at a church in Novato. He called the pastor and asked if he knew where the House of Acts was located so they could visit the site to receive an impartation of the anointing Lonnie carried as a catalyst for the Jesus Movement. The pastor researched it for weeks, but could not find anything on the House of Acts. They finally gave up.

During his time in Novato, Kevin preached at a leadership meeting and told his story of pursuing the mantle of Lonnie Frisbee. During this meeting, a 70-year-old woman stood up. With tears streaming down her face, she said, "I knew Lonnie. I was his art teacher when he was in junior high school. The year Lonnie died, he came to my house. When I opened the door, he looked at me and prophesied, 'When you are seventy years old, there will be a man that comes looking for my mantle, and when he comes give him my mantle, and it will be released to him and to everyone who wants it because Jesus wants to fulfill what He started through me.'"

When Kevin told me that story, I knew the Lord was confirming again the word He had been speaking to me for months regarding my call to be a revivalist and my mandate to raise up a company of revivalists. God is releasing healing revivalists again across the earth, and my mandate is to raise up and release them.

This mandate is directly tied to the hour in which we live. Nothing convinces me more of God's intention to fulfill the prophecy of a billion-soul harvest than seeing Him at work in His Church, preparing not just a few, but everyone who will say *yes* to go to their cities and nations. And they are saying *yes* by the hundreds and thousands. They are inflamed with a commitment to perpetuate an outpouring of His Spirit and are emboldened to travel the earth with remarkable displays of His goodness.

To see God activating the hearts of His people is awesome; even more astounding is that He is installing an entirely new mindset in them—a mentality founded upon the truth that *nothing is impossible.* You'll see how this mindset works in the next chapter.

JESUS CULTURE

CHAPTER 2

THE NEW MINDSET

Aaron McMahon is one of the new breed of revivalist emerging in the earth today. Aaron arrived at Bethel a few years ago to attend the Bethel School of Supernatural Ministry. While he was in school, God not only radically awakened Aaron's heart, He completely rearranged the way he thought. As Aaron began to live from this new revivalist mindset, the Lord started to use him in incredible ways. One of the stories he tells is not just a great testimony, it beautifully illustrates how this new breed thinks. He tells the story in his book, *These Signs Shall Follow:*

On Wednesday, August 1, 2007, I was participating in a business conference call. There were six people on the call—three from my company and three from our client company. As we got started with the call, my partner began by asking Laurie, a woman working for our client company, how her back was doing. Obviously, he was familiar with her situation and was asking for an update. I, on the other hand, knew nothing about this situation. I had never spoken to Laurie before. I expected her to answer my business partner's question with a 15- or 20-second response. When somebody asks you, "Hey, how are you doing?" you typically don't go into every single detail of your life. But Laurie went into great detail for about three or four minutes.

Now I was not exactly supposed to participate in this call. I'm the programmer. For the most part, my job is to sit there quietly and listen. If I hear a technical question, I can jump in and answer it. If my partner thinks I can add something useful without confusing anybody, he'll toss me a softball question to tell me it's okay to talk about something. But essentially, I'm just there to listen to their needs so I can design our software better.

As Laurie went into the second and third minutes of detail, I was becoming amazed at her situation. She wasn't just having back pain; she was having *serious* back problems. She said a disc in her spine was herniated. I don't really understand what that means, but I knew it sounded bad, so it must be bad. She said that another disc was herniated a few years before and she went in for surgery. For the most part, it fixed the problem and her pain level went down. But now, it was back in a different part of her spine and was causing greater problems than the last time. She was losing feeling in her toes and parts of her leg were seriously hurting, apparently due to the way that the nerves travel up the spinal column. Laurie was scheduled for a final pre-surgery appointment the following morning. I'm not sure when her surgery was scheduled, but it sounded like it was going to take place very soon, probably within a couple days. Laurie said she expected to be away from work for eight weeks.

As she gave all these details, I could feel something stirring inside me. I had just graduated from the second year of Bethel School of Supernatural Ministry. "I'm a revivalist. What am I going to do about this situation?" That question burned in me. "What am I going to do?" I had time to debate with myself both sides of the question as Laurie went on for several minutes. I thought, "I'm a revivalist. This is what I do!" But my flesh was saying, "Dude, you're in a business conference call. This is the wrong time and place for prayer!" My spirit responded, "Come on, you just need thirty seconds to get her healed. Thirty seconds! What's that compared to her eight weeks of recovery time?" And my flesh said, "You're going to be in the spotlight with people you don't even know and this is going to be really embarrassing."

This situation put me outside my comfort zone. My flesh wanted just to sit there quietly and hope she would finish soon so I could forget about it. But my destiny burned inside of me. I'm a revivalist. This is what I was born to do—to walk in the footsteps of Jesus and follow His model to bring Him glory. Finally, I made my choice (with a bit of resignation). I thought to myself, "Geeez...I'm a revivalist! I'm going to push all my chips into the center of the table. I know what this is going to cost me in terms of pride and comfort, but it'll be worth it when she's healed and doesn't need to spend eight weeks recovering at home in bed! Thirty seconds of prayer versus eight weeks recovery...I have to do this for her."

So as Laurie was finishing up, I said, "Excuse me, Laurie, I'm Aaron, the programmer. I'm a student in ministry school, and I just can't let this opportunity pass me by. Can I pray for you to be healed? I've seen so many people healed of back issues that I have complete faith for your healing. This will just take thirty seconds."

The conference line got dead quiet. For about three seconds, I heard nothing. Then Laurie said, "Uh, sure. Yes, please pray for me." So I went for it. Granted, it wasn't my most spiritual moment. I felt really "on the spot" and very conscious of the others who were listening in. I tried not to be distracted by imagining what they were probably thinking. At this point, I figured I could call it a success if I could just get through thirty seconds.

I didn't pray for Laurie. Instead, I used the authority given to me by Jesus. I commanded all pain in Laurie's body to leave. I commanded her spinal column and the discs to be realigned by the power of Jesus. I invited more of the Holy Spirit's presence into her body to bring healing and restoration to anything causing problems. I commanded the nerves in her legs and spine to be restored. I released the healing of the blood of Jesus into her. All this took about thirty seconds. I ended with, "Thank you, Jesus. Amen."

Again, there was another long pause. Then I heard nervous laughter from some of the people on the line. Yeah, two years ago before I came to ministry school, even being a passionate Christian then, I probably would have been one of those people nervously laughing, feeling a little embarrassed for the Christian who was taking a huge risk and glad that I wasn't him. I asked Laurie how she felt. She didn't say anything for about four seconds. Then she said, "Wow…*wow!* I feel a lot better! Yeah, I really feel better. I've been in pain all day and now it's gone. The pain's gone."

As I sat alone in my home office, I imagined her moving around and trying it out, then imagined the surprised smile on her face as she realized that this crazy guy's prayer actually worked. I was relieved that it was over. I was *way* outside my comfort zone and I was just happy that I decided to step outside it. Whatever happened from that point on was in God's hands. I took the ball as far as I could take it down the field.

The next morning, I woke up and found an e-mail from Laurie. She was two hours ahead of California time; she'd sent it at 7:00 A.M. my time. She said she was on her way to see her doctor for the pre-surgery appointment and asked for continued prayers. Later on Thursday afternoon, I got an e-mail from her co-worker, who had also been on the conference line. He said that she went to the doctor and told him she was feeling a lot better. He questioned her for a couple minutes to be sure. Then he decided *not* to do the spinal surgery. He knew how difficult the recuperation would be and he wanted any reason not to do it. She agreed. But he told her that this kind of thing doesn't happen often and she should come back if the pain returned. Today, almost two weeks later, Laurie is still doing great. [1]

Did you catch how this new breed thinks differently? I hear these testimonies all the time…stories of the exploits of this new breed that were birthed out of a new way of thinking. Three things stand out to me when I read Aaron's testimony:

1. "Geeez…I'm a revivalist! I'm going to push all my chips into the center of the table. I know what this is going to cost me in terms of pride and comfort, but it'll be worth it when she's healed and doesn't need to spend eight weeks recovering at home in bed! Thirty seconds of prayer versus eight weeks recovery…I have to do this for her."

2. "I didn't pray for Laurie. Instead, I used the authority given to me by Jesus."

3. "I was *way* outside my comfort zone and I was just happy that I decided to step outside it."

This is the new mindset! The new breed of revivalist is willing to lay it all down so the Lord can rise up within them. They push aside selfish ambition, fear, pride, vanity, and the loss of their reputation so that others can encounter the touch of Heaven. They expect Heaven to show up when they take the risk of inviting people to experience God.

Aaron understood his authority and acted on it even though it was inconvenient or could have cost him. You can't suppress someone like this. This new breed is going to be unstoppable. They will be so confident in who they are and so passionate about bringing Heaven to earth that nothing else will matter. They will believe that nothing is impossible and adhere to the words of Jesus: *"...all things are possible to him who believes"* (Mark 9:23). This is an "all things are possible" generation.

Where did Aaron's belief that nothing is impossible come from? Consider another of his statements: "I've seen so many people healed of back issues that I have complete faith for your healing." In my years in Redding and traveling around America and the world, it has become clear to me that the way God is shifting the mindsets of Christians young and old is by *exposing them to the miraculous realm of the Kingdom.*

For example, some time ago our youth group experienced a heightened season in which many people had heavenly encounters and visitations. One of our young men in particular was having powerful times with God, sometimes alone and sometimes when he gathered with friends in his room to seek the Lord. On several of these occasions, they spent most of the night in the presence of God just pressing in for more. The Lord took them into visions, released prophetic dreams to them, and stirred up the realm of the supernatural around their lives.

One evening while they were seeking the Lord, there was a strong sense of His being very close. One of the guys was prophetically painting while another was in the middle of the room praying. All of a sudden, a physical bolt of light shot into the room and struck right in front of the one praying. While the night wore on and they continued to pray, a light began to shine through the window that increased in intensity until they had to close their eyes because they could no longer take the brightness.

We were of course excited to see God showing up in such a significant way among our young people. Linda McIntosh, our high school pastor at the time, asked this young man what God was teaching him through these encounters. His response was priceless. He said, "I am beginning to believe a nation can be saved in a day." This wasn't just some statement he had heard preached and was repeating. His encounters with God had brought him into a new way of thinking about what was possible and had given him faith not only to see but also to be a part of an entire nation turning to God in a day.

WE HAVE THE BALL

This young man's statement was not some grandiose idea about what he wanted to do for God, either. It was simply an acknowledgement that what God commissioned us to do is accessible and achievable.

We are called to disciple nations. This was the mandate Jesus released to us before He ascended to Heaven (see Matt. 28:19). The reason the Church has not stepped into her destiny is that we have not aligned our thinking with His words. For too long, our mindset has been one of inferiority and insignificance, and this attitude has neutralized our anointing to impact nations. We have allowed ourselves to be overwhelmed with the evil state of the world and have believed the lie that we could not make a difference. We have settled for sitting back and letting history happen around us rather than being deliberate in authoring history. We haven't really believed, and thus have not lived, that we are *"the head, and not the tail"* and *"He who is in* [us] *is greater than he who is in the world"* (Deut. 28:13; 1 John 4:4).

In Matthew 28, before Jesus told us to disciple nations, He made it clear that this mandate is feasible because *"All authority has been given to Me in Heaven and on earth"* (Matt. 28:18). Jesus doesn't have all authority just in Heaven; He has it on the earth too. After stating this fact, He said, *"Go therefore,"* thereby giving you and me the keys to that authority (see Matt. 28:19).

Bill Johnson puts it this way: "We have the ball! We are on the offense, not the defense."[2] In sports, coaches design both offensive and defensive plays for their teams to execute. Possession of the ball determines the play a coach will call. He will never call a defensive play when his team has the ball. If a team runs a defensive play when they are on offense, it won't work and they will ultimately lose. Much of the Church has believed that the enemy has the ball, so we are running defensive plays. We have entire playbooks jammed with effective defensive tactics. But these schemes don't work when we have the ball. At times, we've been running the wrong plays. We have given up our authority, constructing our lives to merely endure but not take over.

As a youth pastor, I had the opportunity to speak in Christian clubs on high school campuses. Many times I found that the Christian students were just trying to survive in the midst of a worldly generation. All they knew to do was huddle together, trying to strengthen themselves so they wouldn't fall away. I imagined them gathering each week and saying, "Okay, we made it through one more week, but just barely. Whew! It is bad out there. People are smoking, doing drugs, having sex, and using the Lord's name in vain. I almost didn't make it." Then they would turn to one another and ask, "Are you still saved?" "Yeah, are you still saved?" "Yeah." "Okay, good. Let's meet back here next week to make sure we are still saved." I know that's not what they *really* said, but it's basically what was going on under the surface because of their survival mentality. They were so shaken by the world around them that they weren't contemplating fulfilling the Great Commission. No one had taught them that they had the ball or how to dream and strategize about impacting the entire campus with the Gospel.

But the mindset is shifting. The attitude of the new revivalists is so different because they have realized the truth that they have the ball, and they are learning and running the offensive plays. People are fully engaging in the pursuit of seeing God's glory cover the earth from a place of authority and assurance. They are no longer satisfied to simply exist in the kingdom of the world; they want to see it transfigure into the Kingdom of our God (see Rev. 11:15).

I've been telling young people for years that I want to change the names of Christian clubs to "Pinky and the Brain" clubs. For those who don't know who Pinky and the Brain are, please let me explain. Years ago I used to watch a cartoon show called *Animaniacs*. Part of the show was called "Pinky and the Brain." It was about two mice, one called Pinky and one called Brain. Pinky was a tall, gaunt, dopey-looking mouse that was intellectually challenged. Brain was a short, stocky mouse with a planetary head containing his humongous brain. Every episode was based on the same premise. Pinky and Brain would try to concoct a plan to dominate the world. Their plans were all destined to fail, but at the end of each show, Pinky would turn to Brain and ask this question: "Brain, what are we going to do tomorrow?" With an expression of steely determination, Brain would turn to Pinky and answer with enormous confidence, "We are going to do what we do every day: try to take over the world!"

Pinky and the Brain Clubs. I can see the movement now, fueled by students gathering together to take over the world. Imagine club members Johnny and Cindy, whose dedication is to see their lives radically shake their campus for Jesus. When Johnny is dropped off for school, Cindy is waiting for him. She asks, "Johnny, what are you doing today?" He turns to her with conviction surging in his eyes. "Cindy, I'm going to do what I do every day: try to take over the world!" Just an hour before, Cindy had rolled out of bed and walked into the kitchen to grab some breakfast. As she sat down to eat breakfast, her mom had turned to her and asked, "Honey, what are you up to today?" Cindy had wiped the sleep from her eyes and responded, "Mom, I'm up to the same thing I'm up to every day. I'm going to try to take over the world!"

You are called to take over the world. You are part of a revolution. You are appointed to overthrow the government of darkness that has enslaved people in sin and sickness and to establish the Kingdom of Light on earth as it is in Heaven. Our revolution is not a worldly anarchy of violence and control; it is a Heavenly reformation of *truth* spoken in love and demonstrated in supernatural power. We are armed with uncompromising love and the power of God. You were never created to hide, cowering in some corner, subordinate to evil. Rather, you were born to step out into the midst of plagues of darkness—to stand between the living and the dead and terminate plagues!

You are a plague stopper. Your mandate is not passive, subdued, indifferent, or irrelevant. Jesus freely and unrestrainedly grants to you and me the authority He has been given on the earth.

Christ made another promise when He commissioned us with His authority to disciple nations. He said, *"And lo, I am with you always, even to the end of the age"* (Matt. 28:20). The mindset of the new breed of revivalist is founded upon the awareness that *God is with them*. This is what gives them their sense of significance. If you read the Old Testament, you'll find that every man and woman who performed great exploits for God walked in this revelation.

REVOLUTIONARY

Joshua is a prime example. Joshua was a revolutionary who refused to bow his knee to the lie of insignificance and inferiority. He knew his call was to take over the land promised by God to him and the children of Israel—a rich land, flowing with milk and honey. Before they entered, Moses sent spies ahead to assess the region and its inhabitants. However, the spies returned from their expedition giving Moses a bleak report: the land was full of giants and enemies that could not be defeated.

But Joshua's assessment was completely different. He stood before the people of Israel with confidence fortifying his voice and said:

> *Only do not rebel against the Lord, nor fear the people of the land, **for they are our bread**; their protection has*

departed from them, and the Lord is with us. Do not fear them (Numbers 14:9).

Joshua knew that God was with Israel, and therefore they had the ball. With the Lord on their side, their enemies and all they protected were theirs for the taking. "They are our bread." Now *that's* boldness! With the inspiration that the Lord was with them, Joshua wasn't going to shrink away from His promise into some hidden corner. He was determined to take the land, and he simply viewed the current inhabitants as provision. He had a different perspective—a new breed mindset. He refused to be intimidated by the circumstances or culture or voices around him. He rejected the lie that the world around him was greater than the God who was with him.

The truth is, you cannot impact the world around you if you feel insignificant. At the time of this writing, Brandon Smith is a senior in high school at a top-level school in the San Francisco Bay Area in California. His school has one of the top basketball teams in the nation, and Brandon was on the varsity team as a freshman—the youngest player on the team.

Early one morning after a practice, Brandon was in the locker room dressing for school when the senior captain of the team, along with other teammates, approached him and his friend (who was the only other freshmen on the team). The captain of the team asked Brandon if he was a virgin. Without shrinking back at all, Brandon proudly proclaimed, "Yes, I am a virgin. And I am proud of that. It is something that is precious to me, and I am saving it until my marriage." The team was shocked at his answer and looked at him like he was crazy. There was even chuckling as the guys walked away. During that day, different young men came up and told him how much they respected his decision and how they wish they had done the same. But the label of *virgin* stuck with him throughout his high school years, so much so that a couple of years later at a game with their local rival school, Brandon was on the free throw line and the student crowd was chanting, "He's a virgin! He's a virgin!" Brandon said he wanted to shout back, "I'm proud of it! I'm proud of it!"

God truly is raising up a new breed who refuse to believe they are insignificant. Brandon knew he wasn't called to just survive and be ashamed of who he was. He was called to stand out, not fit in. Even though he was nervous, and even though he knew it could cost him approval from his peers, he accepted that it was worth it. Brandon felt secure in his identity in God and had no need for others to tell him who he was. He had established his life in intimacy with the Lord and was not agitated by the pressure to seek acceptance or relevance in the eyes of the world. I will cover the importance of intimacy and identity in a later chapter.

HEALING THE LAND

This assertive shift from defense to offense forces us to reconsider what ministry looks like. If the goal is survival, then ministry is mostly focused on taking care of the flock and somewhat focused on getting people saved. This was the common understanding of ministry when I was growing up and first became a youth pastor. "Working for the Lord" meant becoming a pastor or evangelist and exercising the gift of standing behind a pulpit or a crusade platform, teaching the Word of God to a congregation. It was generally assumed that any young people who showed signs of passion for God or leadership skills should be pastors.

In the last ten years, however, as the Church has begun to recognize and embrace our true commission, there has been a major shift in the way we view ministry. When the goal is to disciple nations, transform society, and see the glory of the Lord cover the earth, then ministry at the very least has to be happening outside church buildings as much as inside them, if not more. Christian ministry must address every aspect of human life.

THE SEVEN

In 1975, Bill Bright and Loren Cunningham both had similar

visions from the Lord that provide us with a key for shaping nations.[3] One of them saw seven "mountains" (high places), and the other saw seven "mind molders" (spheres of influence) in society. For their ministry and generation, the Lord highlighted the places they were to emphasize—whoever would influence those mountains and mind molders in turn would shape society and transform their culture. God has continued to speak to us about the need to impact the mountains with Kingdom wisdom and love and joy and power. We talk about the mountains of culture in the following categories or institutions:

- Family
- Religion
- Economy
- Education
- Government
- Arts and media
- Science and technology

The vision is simple. Whoever commands and controls those mountains sets the agenda and atmosphere in a society.

Lance Wallnau, who is one of the foremost authorities on the Seven Mountains, says this:

> Loren saw seven strategic mountains of influence that shape the minds of the people or the culture of every nation. God told him that if His people could capture these strategic places, there would be marketplace transformation and they would reap the harvest of nations.[4]

He continues by saying:

> God gave us the understanding of these spheres to guide us in carrying out the Great Commission of

Matthew 28—to disciple nations for Him. The true fulfillment of the Great Commission will bring people into
a complete experience of the Kingdom of God that
includes godly economic systems, Bible-based forms of
government, education anchored in God's Word, families with Jesus at the head, entertainment that portrays
God in His variety and excitement, media that is based
on communicating the truth in love, and churches that
serve as sending stations for missionaries into all areas
of society. He says to occupy until He comes. To occupy
means to take leadership.[5]

God is giving the Church a prescription to bring in the harvest
and, ultimately, to *heal the land*. God is intent on giving the nations
of the earth to His Son as His inheritance. His desire is to see the
nations of the earth turn from being cursed to being healed and
blessed. This desire must shape our understanding of our role as
revivalists. Our goal is not simply to get people healed, delivered,
and saved; it is to bring reformation and restoration to the "ruined
cities" (see Isa. 61:4).

God gave us one strategy for healing the land in Chronicles:

*If My people who are called by My name will humble them-
selves, and pray and seek My face, and turn from their
wicked ways, then I will hear from Heaven, and will forgive
their sin and heal their land* (2 Chronicles 7:14).

Malachi gave us another strategy when he prophesied that the
hearts of the fathers and sons being turned to one another would
keep the land from being cursed (see Mal. 4:5-6). I will address this
subject further in the next two chapters.

We find a third strategy in the story of Elisha, whose first
miracle after receiving the mantle of Elijah was to heal the water
near Jericho:

Then the men of the city said to Elisha, "Please notice, the situation of this city is pleasant, as my lord sees; but the water is bad, and the ground barren." And he said, "Bring me a new bowl, and put salt in it." So they brought it to him. Then he went out to the source of the water, and cast in the salt there, and said, "Thus says the Lord: 'I have healed this water; from it there shall be no more death or barrenness.'" So the water remains healed to this day, according to the word of Elisha which he spoke (2 Kings 2:19-22).

Through this miracle, Jericho went from being cursed to being blessed by God. I believe that this miracle is a parable of the blueprint God gave to Bill Bright and Loren Cunningham for affecting the sources of influence in society. The land of Jericho was barren because the water was stale, but it became fruitful when the water was healed. Likewise, the barrenness or fruitfulness of cities and nations is determined by what flows from the seven mountains and mind molders. Elisha's strategy was to take a new bowl and throw salt into the sources of the water, and this resulted in the water being restored to its original purpose and the land becoming fruitful. God is releasing a new strategy (new bowl) as He is throwing believers (salt) into the sources of water in society.

The new breed of revivalist emerging in the earth today will not only stand behind pulpits but will also step into every realm of society to heal the water so the land may be fruitful and blessed. It is from the peaks of those seven mountains that the sources of water flow down through society to nourish it either for good or evil, to bless or to curse. For too long, the Church has only validated those who have entered into traditional church ministry and not realized that God wants to take *every* believer (the salt of the earth) and throw them into the very sources of water in nations to regenerate our land.

At Jesus Culture conferences, this is one of our missions—not just to raise up preachers, but revivalists who are CEOs of multibillion-dollar companies; mothers who start up homes for unwed mothers;

social workers who change the way we take care of our children; politicians who make laws that reflect the counsel of the Lord; judges who extend the scepter of God's justice in the earth; authors who write books that reveal the nature and character of God to a nation; screenwriters who write movies that compel us to action for good; and principals who uncover better methods to educate students.

During one of our conferences, Cindy Jacobs pulled me aside and said, "Banning, you must find out who you have in your midst." There are more than just preachers among us: there are white-hot revivalists who will transform culture through resuscitating all seven realms of society.

Radical, fervent, healing revivalists, called to impact cultures for the Kingdom of God, are being commissioned to rehabilitate the land. As part of the new breed, you must pay attention to the dreams in your heart because they are meaningful to God. Don't downplay the desires of your heart. God will use them to place you in society as an agent of restoration.

The revelation that we are called to minister in society has expanded my understanding of what it looks like for the glory of the Lord to rise on His people. Obviously, it means that we are to take the healing ministry of Christ into our workplaces, schools, and businesses, like Aaron did. But it is more than that. Every aspect of our lives is to manifest the superior reality of the Kingdom. The Kingdom of God contains the wisdom and resources for making us successful in every area of life. Kings and nations will be drawn to the brightness of our rising as we, the Church, display God's wisdom in everything we do. Of course, the point of God throwing revivalists into every realm of society is not just so Christians can be better than the world. I want Christians to make the finest movies in Hollywood, not just so we can say we have the most talented filmmakers in the industry but for the superlative purpose of seeing this nation healed and blessed.

I know people who are revivalists in different realms of society. Chris Adams is the superintendent of a school district in California.

Kelly Clark is an Olympic and X Games gold medalist. Shaun Alexander is a former MVP in the National Football League. Scott Reynolds is a writer in Hollywood. Jeremy Edwardson is the lead singer of the rock band, The Myriad. Bill Ostan is a lawyer in the military. George Scripture is a social worker. Andrew Sievright is a businessman who has started the largest orphanage and school in Kenya. All of these men and women are revivalists whom God is using to heal our land.

The fun part is that all these people are doing what they love to do *and* being used by God. God rarely sends you to Africa if you don't have a heart for the African nations. God prefers to access the passions of *your* heart because your aspiration is an essential ingredient for excellence in whatever field you pursue. God wants to anoint your inclinations and yearnings with the fire and purpose of Heaven. The convergence between our individual abilities and passions with the call upon our lives is what makes us "salty" and gives us our potency to bring change and healing in society.

This is why part of my job in raising up this new breed of revivalist is to help them identify the dreams in their hearts and call them to excellence and leadership. For too many years, the idea has persisted that God wants us to be mindless servants who don't get to think or care about anything except reading our Bibles and going to church. But as part of the new breed, you must pay attention to the dreams and desires in your heart, because they will help you get in touch with the invitation God is extending to you to partner with Heaven and bring healing to the land. As Bill Johnson preaches, "Most of the Church is waiting for the next command from God, but God is waiting for the dream of His Church."[6]

Kelly Clark is not only one of the most dominant female snowboarders in the world, but she is a radical revivalist. As I mentioned before, she has won numerous competitions, including an Olympic Gold Medal and an X Games Gold Medal. The Lord hand-picked her and placed her like salt in the extreme sports world to bring healing to the land. Through her life, people are regularly encountering the love and power of God. Consistently, her fellow teammates call her when they need healing because she has a reputation when she prays for people. People are encountering God through her life.

Not only is she impacting people on a personal level, she is impacting the entire snowboarding culture. The favor on her life is crazy. She designed her own Burton snowboard on which she put Scriptures and prophetic art. She was recently part of a team that made a high level snowboarding movie, which documents the lives of a few Christian riders. At the first showing, 65 people gave their lives to Jesus. Even her board boldly declares her love for Jesus. Kelly is a shining example of what God intends to do in a generation. He is raising up revivalists whom He will send into every realm of society to bring healing to the land.

You may not feel like your life can make a difference, but you are a major part of God's plan for the nations of the earth. I once heard Iverna Tompkins, one of my favorite preachers and a woman who inspired me to become a preacher, say, "I may just be a drop in the bucket, but the bucket isn't full until I'm in it."

Your life is critically potent with the plans of God. The dreams ingrained upon your heart are resident there because God wants to use you to bring revival in the particular realm of society you are zealous about. In fact, God has set it up so that His dream of giving the nations to His Son as well as the dreams of His sons and daughters can only be fulfilled together. The passions of your heart are intimately and intrinsically linked to God's desire for nations being discipled and societies completely transformed!

You have been set up for success. God is with you, and nothing is impossible.

SECTION II

UNDER COVERING

THE PRIMARY FOUNDATION stone for this whole new breed of revivalist is when the rod (representative of the authority of Moses) and the sword (signifying the courage and skill of Joshua) come together for worldwide revival. Without the alignment of these generations—working together for the common cause of seeing God's Kingdom come—we will flounder about in the weakness of independence and make ourselves vulnerable to the enemy's divisive strategies.

There is often much frustration, disappointment, and criticism between the generations, which is consequently inhibiting the fulfillment of God's purposes in and through both generations. Without the submission of the younger generation in honoring their spiritual parents, and without the empowerment and releasing of the older generation toward the younger generation, we won't be able to sustain the strength and increase that accompanies a culture bound by humility, unity, and trust.

Covering brings benefits! Faithfulness has its rewards. Learn the blessings that come with the power of God's ordered alignment: the inheritance of courage, wisdom, identity, protection, and an anointing for signs and wonders. You don't need to spend your life striving on your own when you can build upon what your fathers and mothers have already established. The choice is yours.

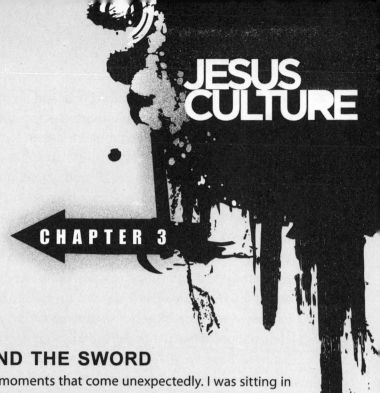

CHAPTER 3

THE ROD AND THE SWORD

It was one of those moments that come unexpectedly. I was sitting in an airport in Texas on my way to a meeting in Colorado Springs when the Lord showed me something that would change my life forever. As I waited to board the plane, I read Exodus 17:8-16, which is the story of Moses holding up his hands as Joshua fought the Amalekites. I discovered that things I had been learning for years about the generations coming together suddenly clicked into place to form a complete picture. (I love those moments when the puzzle pieces of revelation connect and I get to see a more complete panorama of what the Lord has been creating in my life.) I had been mobilizing and equipping young revivalists in their teens and twenties for years, but sitting there in the airport I saw the primary foundation stone for a whole new breed of revivalist. This breed would be established as *the rod and the sword come together for* worldwide revival. I'll clarify what I mean in a moment.

I was on my way to Colorado Springs at the invitation of my friend, Bill Ostan. Bill was heading up the youth "arm" of Generals International, Mike and Cindy Jacob's ministry. He had called me to see if I would come out for a few days to brainstorm with about

30 other young leaders, plus Lou Engle and Cindy Jacobs, on how to ignite a prayer movement on campuses across the nation. A few days after I received his invitation, I had a dream that set me up for the puzzle pieces to come together.

In the dream, my wife SeaJay and I were in Colorado Springs at the World Prayer Center. I had never been to the World Prayer Center or Colorado Springs before, but in the dream I knew that's where we were, and I remember admiring how enormous and beautiful the building was. SeaJay and I entered and began to look for the meeting with Cindy and Lou to discuss this campus prayer movement. We wandered down different halls and eventually found the gathering in a room with amphitheater-style seating. As I walked in, I immediately noticed a few things. First, there were far more than 30 young leaders—there were a little over a hundred. Second, all of the people in the room were younger than me (I was 24 years old at the time). Third, Lou Engle and Cindy Jacobs were not there.

SeaJay and I found our way to seats in the front row and sat down. As we waited for the proceedings to begin, I could feel a sense of chaos and confusion in the room. The leader of the meeting, a young man in his early twenties, started by asking if anyone wanted to share a testimony. What happened next took me completely by surprise. Instead of testifying, the young people began to stand and mock and taunt one another, hurling insults back and forth. I recall it so clearly. One girl stood up and responded to what someone had said to her by shouting back, "Oh yeah? Well, you have a big butt." It was pure craziness, and it didn't take long before my frustration level peaked.

What I seemed to know instinctively was the reason for the confusion and chaos in the meeting: sons were talking to sons, and daughters were talking to daughters, and the fathers and mothers had not shown up!

Utterly frustrated, SeaJay and I rose to leave. As we stepped into the hallway, the leader came after us and said, "Please stay; we need you." I turned to him and said, "If the fathers and mothers of this thing don't show up, I don't have time to be here!"

After I received that dream, I knew I was supposed to go to the meeting. However, even after I had my "airport revelation" on the way to Colorado Springs, I had yet to find out how the dream and the revelation were connected and why God was speaking to me. When I arrived in Colorado Springs, I went directly to the church where the meeting was to be held, excited to discuss with other leaders how to ignite youth prayer on campuses. As I entered the sanctuary, I noticed right away that there were more than 30 leaders in attendance. Just as in my dream, there were a little over a hundred people, and the majority of them were younger than I was. I knew all of them were there because they were hungry for God and passionate about His Kingdom. After the first session, Lou and I sat down for lunch. During the course of our conversation, Lou asked what the Lord had been showing me. I briefly shared my "airport revelation," and he asked me to deliver it to the group that night.

The evening meeting began with worship, and then Cindy Jacobs spoke for a few minutes. She started by asking an incredibly relevant question for the Church in our nation, and framed it by quoting statistics that reveal that churches in America are holding on to only 10 percent of their young people after they turn 18. In other words, 90 percent of our young people leave their churches when they become adults—a staggering and sobering statistic.

Then she asked us this question: "What can we do to keep our young people from leaving the church?"

For the next hour and a half, young people responded by sharing their frustrations with the older generation. They talked about how they thought the older generation needed to change in order to keep them in church. "They need to change the music. They need to turn the lights down during worship. They need to value us more if they expect us to stay around."

The criticism went on for a while. I sat there grieved at what I was hearing, but I understood even more of my dream and the revelation I had received at the airport. These were outstanding young leaders who loved the Lord with all of their hearts, yet their responses were affected by a frame of mind that put them at odds with the older generation. There was no time for me to share that evening, so Lou asked me to speak the following morning.

The next morning, I communicated what the Lord had been downloading about the generations being in proper alignment. I told them about my personal journey and the revelation I had received about the younger generation aligning under the older generation. As I was talking, I could sense the Holy Spirit confirming what I was saying to others. The same revelation that had hit me began to affect others. And in the exact room where young people had expressed their frustration with the older generation the night before, perspectives began to shift.

After I sat down, Dutch Sheets, the senior pastor of the church where we were meeting, got up to share. He said, "The seeds that killed the Jesus Movement were in this room last night." That was astounding to me. As I've mentioned, at 24 I had already developed a love for and knowledge of revival history and was very familiar with the Jesus Movement, which was an incredible revival with a monumental impact. It was not sustained, however, and I believe it ended prematurely.

After this statement, the younger people all over the room began to repent from the way they had been viewing the older generation. It was a powerful time as the young leaders humbled themselves and gave honor to the older generation. The *rod* and the *sword* were aligning.

MOSES AND JOSHUA

Let me explain what I shared at the Colorado Springs gathering in more depth, beginning with my "airport revelation." The passage in Exodus 17 is a powerful story. It is where we first meet Joshua, the future leader of the people of Israel, and it gives us an important insight into the relationship between Moses and Joshua.

Briefly, the context for this story is as follows. When the Israelites left Egypt, they plundered the people of Egypt. Thus, when they entered the wilderness, they possessed an abundance of gold and other valuable items. This provoked many of the surrounding nations to initiate fights with them in the hope of getting their hands on some of the wealth. The Amalekites were one group that knew about the Israelites' affluence and provoked them into battle.

The story begins with Moses telling Joshua to select some men to fight the Amalekites. As Joshua led the army into war, Moses carried the rod of God up to the top of the hill overlooking the battle. He positioned himself with his hands raised, firmly grasping the rod of God. As long as Moses kept his hands outstretched, Joshua was victorious. But Moses eventually began to grow weary and drop his hands. When his hands were down, the battle shifted and Joshua and his men began to be defeated. So Aaron and Hur rallied around Moses and propped his hands up until Joshua's victory was complete.

In his commentary on this story, John Wesley, referring to the people of Israel, said, "The hand of Moses contributed more to their safety than their own hands."[1] Joshua's victory was completely dependent on Moses being in position with the rod of God. As great a warrior as Joshua was, and as well-trained and ready as his men were, the deciding factor in the battle was not Joshua's skill in combat, but Moses' authority represented by the rod of God. When Moses was out of position, even though Joshua and his men were fighting with the same proficiency and intensity, the battle shifted and they began to be defeated. Joshua was triumphant because he was properly aligned with Moses, the older generation. Victory was not dependent on the sword in the hands of Joshua, the younger generation, but on the rod in the hands of Moses, the older generation. Nor was the victory dependent solely on Moses. He needed Aaron, Hur, and Joshua to step into victory as a tribe.

The rod, in the life of Moses and throughout Scripture, represents authority, power, and leadership, while the sword is used to administer the work of the Lord. The covering of authority provided by an older leader was essential to the young leader's success in fulfilling the task at hand.

In order to understand the lesson of this story, I need to point out that there are two spiritual principles at work here, which are distinct but related. The first principle is submission to authority, and the second is young people honoring their elders.

SUBMISSION

The principle of submission to authority is simply that all people, in every generation, are called to be under authority. In fact, we cannot walk in authority without being submitted under authority. The centurion who asked Jesus to heal his servant understood that Jesus had authority because He was surrendered to God, just as the centurion was *"a man under authority"* and could therefore commission his servants to do what he said (see Matt. 8:8-9). The apostle Paul modeled submission to authority. In his early years of ministry he was submitted under Barnabas, and when he was sent out on his missionary journeys he was commissioned by James and the council at Jerusalem. He did not go out on his own as an apostle who didn't need input from others; he submitted his ministry and was sent by the apostles.

Submission to authority is to be ongoing throughout our lives, no matter how long we have held a role of authority. When I became a father, I didn't stop being a son. Both of these functions work simultaneously in my life.

I feel it is important to clarify here that submitting to authority is different from honoring our elders because there isn't a special age where the Lord entrusts someone with a rod. I have seen people in their twenties who walk in a measure of authority and carry the rod, and I have observed people in their forties who desperately need to find covering and do not carry the rod of God.

There are cases where God raises up a young leader to provide a covering of authority over many who are older than he or she, and those people come under that covering by submitting to the younger person. However, I do think there is experience and wisdom that can only come from years lived. The reason most people in authority are older is that they have proved to be capable of carrying the rod through years of experience.

HONOR

The principle of honoring our elders, particularly our fathers and mothers, is clearly taught in Scripture. The fourth commandment states, *"Honor your father and your mother, that your days may be long upon the land which the Lord your God is giving you"* (Exod. 20:12). At Bethel, we summarize the principle contained in this commandment very simply: Life flows through honor. There is a current of life—a continuity of power and blessing—that only comes to us when we actively honor our parents, natural and spiritual alike.

The reason I believe God showed me the story in Exodus is that both these elements—submission to authority and honor between the generations—were in operation. There was a combined release of authority and blessing in the midst of the battle because of the way Joshua and Moses interacted. The result of their convergence was victory.

I have been in youth and young adult ministry for well over a decade and am thoroughly convinced that the younger generation needs to understand covering and spiritual authority and that it is imperative to be connected to spiritual mothers and fathers if we are going to be victorious. No matter how well I train the younger generation, my efforts will be wasted if they are not properly joined with the older generation. They may be exceptional with the sword, but if they aren't connected with the rod their triumph will be fleeting. The rod is in the hands of the "Moses generation"—the older generation—and it must be partnered with the sword, which is in the hands of the "Joshua generation." I believe this alliance is a vital key to seeing revival sustained in this generation of the Body of Christ.

By saying that we must come under the rod in the hands of the older generation, I am not negating the fact that, despite our age or maturity level, authority has been given to every believer by Christ to heal the sick, cast out demons, and move in power. Christ is the ultimate authority that we are all called to come under, and doing so qualifies us to walk in the authority He gives us. However, I do not believe Christ automatically entrusts all of us with the authority to take cities and see nations turn to God. It is my opinion that He entrusts certain people with that authority, and this is why I am giving my life to raise up a new breed of revivalist who will offer themselves for worldwide revival—revivalists who will see entire cities and nations saved and brought under the dominion of the King.

But there is a process of maturity these revivalists must experience in order to stand in that place of authority, a process which will not be complete without the blessing, teaching, impartation, and covering of mothers and fathers. I cannot send a new breed of revivalist into battle without making certain they have the authority necessary to be victorious both in their personal lives and in their assignment in worldwide revival.

Let me address this point briefly. I believe the Lord wants to release an authority on the Church to see entire cities saved and nations discipled. But God has always called us to live a conquering life on the inside as well. We can only *consistently* release the Kingdom of God to those around us to the degree that the Kingdom is established in our own lives. For this reason, I cannot separate calling a generation to impact nations from calling them to fully embrace what the Lord has for them—a life of true freedom from those things that hinder our destiny as world-changers—*"the sin that so easily entangles"* us (Heb. 12:1 NIV). Personal victory also comes through proper participation with those who hold the rod of God. God is calling this new breed of revivalist to walk in power *and* display the character of God, and both are achieved through submitting to covering.

You need the authority of godly, mature mothers and fathers in order to establish a life of holiness and purity. I see many young people struggling with issues of sin or areas of weakness, and they cannot gain victory because they are hiding in shame or fear of punishment from the fathers and mothers in their lives. They are not necessarily living from an evil heart, but they feel trapped and powerless to withstand temptation. As God brings the generations together and these young people connect with fathers and mothers, power-lessness will be replaced with the strength and grace that begins to flow in their lives. We will see young people living successfully in holi-ness and purity.

INDEPENDENCE

The generation gap in the church today is real, and it is hurting us. I believe there are two main reasons for this. One is a spirit of inde-pendence in the generations. The second is an incorrect emphasis on how revival is going to come. First let me address the spirit of inde-pendence in the Church.

There is something inside the younger generation that wants to do things without the help of others. You are either currently young or have been at one point in time, so you understand this. The major-ity of the younger generation doesn't think the older generation understands them. Especially in the Western World, most can't wait until they're of legal age to have the freedom to do things their own way. This paradigm widens the generational gap and separates the sword from the rod.

However, the spirit of independence is not exclusive to young people. It also exists in the older generation. The older generation in many ways finds the younger simply frustrating. My parents were raised in a different era, and many people younger than I am confuse them. Obviously, I am not addressing choices to sin; those are griev-ous to any generation. Rather, I am addressing style. They simply have a hard time understanding why anyone would listen to that genre of music, or decorate their body with tattoos and piercings, or appreciate the variety of different things that young people embrace. Even at 32, I find myself puzzled by some of what the younger generation does. It gets more and more challenging for the older generation to relate to the younger, so the generation gap widens and the true strength of the Church operating as one generation is never fully realized. This division between the generations in the Church will hinder revival.

Joshua's lack of a spirit of independence allowed him to be properly aligned in relationship with Moses. The Bible says, *"Joshua did as Moses said to him…"* (Exod. 17:10). Joshua was not out there looking to do his own thing. His obedience positioned him under the covering of Moses and declared that he understood the significance of covering. Moses, for his part, accepted the importance of empowering the generation coming after him and trusted Joshua as he released him to battle.

Ultimately, independence is dangerous because it is grounded in *pride*. First Peter says:

> *Likewise you younger people, submit yourselves to your elders. Yes, all of you be submissive to one another, and be clothed with humility, for **"God resists the proud, but gives grace to the humble"*** (1 Peter 5:5).

When the younger generation wants to do their own thing and resists submitting to the older generation, they are essentially saying, "We think we can do it better." Now, that's pride.

When the older generation shuts down the younger generation, they are essentially saying, "We don't need you. We don't trust you. Come back when you are older." And that is also pride.

God's command is to submit and to *"be clothed with humility"* because submission is an act of humility. When a person humbles himself, grace begins to flow into his life. But if a person refuses to humble himself, God will oppose the pride in his life. There is an entire generation in the Church that is in danger of having God oppose them, unless they can submit to their elders and to one another and clothe themselves with humility. But this step will require a shift in the way we've been viewing things—a transformation that had to happen in my own life.

I had a spirit of independence on me as a young man. Of course I didn't realize it, but it was there. As I mentioned, I was raised in a loving Christian home and started full-time ministry at 19. Like many young people, I grew up with no understanding of the importance of spiritual authority. It wasn't until Kris Vallotton came into my life that I began to recognize the spirit of independence manipulating my life and the negative impact it was having on me.

Kris arrived at Bethel a couple of years after I came on staff and not only became my boss but a father in my life. One day he called me into his office and, as only Kris can do, told me I was independent. I sat there reeling for a moment because I was certain he was wrong.

I'm not independent, I thought. *I'm confident. I just know where I am headed in life and that makes me sure of myself.*

In my mind I desperately tried to defend myself. But as he continued to talk to me, a light came on. A part of my life I had never seen before, a major blind spot, was no longer in the dark. I was autonomous. I was not connected with fathers and mothers. I was doing my own thing, self-sufficient, and building my own ministry apart from covering.

As it struck me like a two-ton weight, I began to weep. I'm not sure why I had never perceived it before. If I had glimpsed it before I probably thought it was a sign of strength and maturity. But I recognized it when Kris pointed it out. I also knew that it wasn't my heart's desire to be separate. I just had no idea how to allow fathers and mothers into my life at that level, how to submit to covering, or how to align myself under spiritual authority. It was nothing I had ever fully done.

Even though I wasn't sure where to begin learning how to do these things, that afternoon I committed to do them. I had no idea how hard it might be or the testing I might have to go through. But I knew that the spirit of independence had separated me from the rod. I was isolated and had to establish a high value for and attachment to the rod if I were to fulfill my destiny.

WRONG EMPHASIS

The second contributing factor to the generation gap in the Church today is a wrong emphasis on how revival comes. A couple of years before my trip to Colorado Springs, we had a season at Bethel during which visiting speakers called those under 25 years of age to come forward and prayed for them, declaring revival was coming through the youth. "Revival is coming through the youth" became a common phrase to us.

Shortly after we started hearing this, Kris Vallotton got up in a service and said, "Revival is not coming through the young people." At first I was offended by this statement and didn't know what to make of it. I knew that in many cases historically God used young people to spark revival. That was one of the reasons I was working with them, and it is still. However, I also knew that revival, for the most part, has never lasted past one generation (the Jesus Movement being one of the most recent examples). Many people have explained this by pointing out that God is sovereign and comes and goes as He pleases. This has furnished the belief that we don't have any influence over when revival comes or leaves. But our revelation of God's intention for revival was changing—we were beginning to see that He meant it not only to be sustained from generation to generation, but to increase.

I knew we had to do something different if we were going to see revival perpetuate past one generation, so I listened intently to Kris, who was insistent that revival was not coming through young people. He described an encounter in which the Lord spoke to him and said, "Revival is not coming through the youth; it's coming through one generation." Kris began to teach that revival would come as the generations united together, and because of this we need to be on guard against the divisive strategies of the enemy. Satan knows he can't stop this move of God, so he is dividing the generations to bring a curse on the land. This message brought me to the realization that one of my main mandates in ministry is to join the generations to see worldwide revival.

After Kris exposed the divisive strategy of the enemy, I began to see it at work in the older generation. The emphasis on the youth and revival was subtly sending a message to the older generation that their days of being used by God in revival were over or were quickly passing. If that were true, at most they might be able to stand on the sidelines and sow finances into revival, but otherwise they could only watch the young people God was going to utilize for revival. They began to feel redundant and despondent as we pursued an outpouring of God's Spirit. If the Holy Spirit had not restored the message that called them to their rightful purpose, the enemy might have succeeded in benching half the players in the game. The truth is that we desperately need the older generation, and they are called to very active roles in revival. They hold the rod of God, and their greatest days of impact for the Kingdom are ahead of them.

I also saw this strategy at work years ago in a youth pastors' meeting where a youth pastor spoke up and said, "The older generation needs to get out of the way and let the youth have their revival. The older generation is too set in their ways to change. They need to move over so we can have our revival." Unfortunately, I have often been confronted with this attitude over the years, but thankfully I am seeing change. We shouldn't want the older generation to get out of the way; we need them to take their place of leadership in revival with the authority the Lord has given them. I tell youth pastors, "We don't have a choice. The generations must be aligned if we are to see the revival that has been prophesied. We need the rod of God in our lives and they need the sword in their lives."

I need to say that the idea that this pastor expressed, that the older generation is too set in their ways, is a lie. If you come to Bethel on any Sunday you will see the most radical, crazy, zealous "old" people you've ever seen. They love the new style of worship. They love this move of God. They are some of the first people to rush the stage for prayer. They come early and leave late. They walk in power, prophesy over anything that moves, and dive headfirst into the river of God. In fact, there was a season when I looked around our church and noticed that the most radical, zealous, on-fire Christians were not young people. They were the "old folks."

I had to encourage our young people to try and keep up with the adults. Lou Engle once said, "I may be fifty years old, but you're going to have to run hard to keep up with me." That's the way it's supposed to be. The older generation may not have the physical energy and stamina of the younger generation, but their fire is hotter than ever.

Likewise, the idea that those in the younger generation don't value the older generation and only care about themselves is also untrue. I know that there are reasons these stereotypes have developed (the unchanging older generation and the selfish younger generation). But they are not the rule, and they have not been my experience. I see so many young people whose heart is to honor the older generation and to follow their lead as they pursue revival.

Recently, our youth group took up an offering for Diamond Fellowship, the ministry to seniors at Bethel Church. A group from Diamond Fellowship was going to Mexico on a mission trip to preach, lay hands on the sick, and bring the Kingdom. Our youth wanted to honor them and support them as they headed off to change the world. It is time for the generations to join. But it must be done with proper alignment.

God has set up an order for relationship between the generations, and we cannot bypass it. As I studied the concept of the generations aligning in Scripture, I was drawn, along with the relationship between Moses and Joshua, to the relationships between Mordecai and Esther and between Elijah and Elisha. It has been prophesied over the younger generation that they are a Joshua generation who will inherit the Promised Land, that they are an Esther generation who will stand before the King and see a nation saved, and that they are an Elisha generation who will operate in a double-portion anointing. I believe those prophecies with all of my heart. But each of those people had one thing in common. They were all appropriately aligned with the older generation. Joshua followed Moses, Elisha served Elijah, and Esther listened to Mordecai, even when she was queen. As a young revivalist, I cannot just do my own thing and hope to be successful.

I need to follow God's pattern and be taught from the example of Joshua, Esther, and Elisha.

Sons and daughters were never intended to direct fathers and mothers. Fathers and mothers were meant to guide. Certainly one of the ways they lead is by equipping and commissioning sons and daughters and building avenues for their dreams to be fulfilled. However, they do not empower by stepping aside but by running together. In order to run together, there must be genuine honor in their hearts for one another.

FINDING MOTHERS AND FATHERS

I have been speaking generally of the "younger generation" being aligned with the "older generation," but hopefully you can see that I am speaking specifically of young believers coming into submitted relationships with mature, trustworthy spiritual mothers and fathers. I was talking about this subject of covering and submitting to fathers and mothers with a friend of mine who has a very influential world-wide ministry. He pointed out that I come from a healthy culture where the leaders are not controlling and are *for* me. Not everyone comes from that type of environment, as I have come to realize after spending many hours with young people and young leaders wherever I travel. He asked what I thought they should do. To be honest, I have no easy answers. But I know for certain that the Lord looks at the heart. If young people and young leaders can put fathers and mothers in a place of honor in their hearts, the rest will work out. I believe the Lord can keep you from the spirit of independence even if you don't presently have great mothers and fathers in your life.

However, the lack of strong spiritual mothers and fathers in this generation is an indication that this message must impact both the younger and older generations. Malachi says that God will *"turn the hearts of the fathers to the children, and the hearts of the children to their fathers"* (Mal. 4:6). Notice that the hearts of the fathers turn first, and then the hearts of the children turn. I do believe the hearts of the older generation must turn to the younger generation. If you are in a situation where that hasn't happened yet, my advice once again is to make sure that your heart is in a place of honor. You may not be in control of others, but you are certainly in control of yourself. Pray and ask God to raise up mothers and fathers in your life, and position your heart to receive those He brings to you.

Joshua, Esther, and Elisha immensely valued the men who provided their spiritual covering. As each one of these giants in the faith discovered and as we will explore in the following chapter, covering brings blessings into your life that you could never receive any other way.

JESUS CULTURE

CHAPTER 4

THE POWER OF ALIGNMENT

Covering comes with some great benefits. Early in ministry I learned that if I align my heart and life with mature men and women of God—fathers and mothers—then I receive what they have. If I honor in my heart those the Lord has placed over my life, I am privileged to occupy the ground they've fought for. The Bible calls this *inheritance,* a concept that is somewhat lost in our society but is nonetheless a powerful biblical principle.

I've been extremely blessed with some great fathers and mothers in my life—not only my natural parents but also spiritual parents. People like Bill Johnson, Kris Vallotton, Danny Silk, Dann Farrelly, Lou Engle, Cindy Jacobs, and many others have poured into my life. Some of my fathers and mothers have invested in me on a close, personal level and some from a distance as I have observed their lives and been enhanced and empowered by their teaching. As I drew close to these great men and women of God, I was blown away by the things they had gained in the Spirit—revelations the Lord had given them, insights into Scripture, wisdom for life, and keys for successful and victorious living. *Inheritance* means I acquire what they have gained. What they have comes my way because I have aligned myself under their covering.

The names I just mentioned, the fathers and mothers in my life, might be familiar to you. However, I don't mean to imply that the mothers and fathers in your life all have to be prominent leaders in the Body of Christ. I had the privilege of overseeing the second-year program of Bethel School of Supernatural Ministry for four years. Students of all ages apply to the school from around the world to be trained and equipped for revival, and most of them come because they have read Bill Johnson's books or heard Kris Vallotton speak.

Over those four years, I noticed that when they came to the school and heard the teaching on the importance of fathers and mothers, many of them wanted Bill and Kris to father them. Because Bill and Kris were the most visible leaders, students placed a higher value on them than others in the Body of Christ who are also fathers and mothers. This is understandable; Bill and Kris are amazing men who have an incredible relationship with God and walk in a high level of anointing. However, Bill and Kris are only two men. They generously give away their inheritance of wisdom and anointing to all who will listen, but they cannot personally disciple more than a few.

What I teach people is that God has ordained men and women to release the benefits of covering in your life, but not all of the people He has assigned to you will be "famous." The fathers and mothers in my life, both the ones you would and wouldn't know, were all arranged by God. They are God-ordained relationships. Some of the greatest fathers and mothers you can align under may not be well known. Kris Vallotton's spiritual father is a godly man full of wisdom who helped shape Kris into the man he is today, but most people wouldn't know who Bill Derryberry is. There are men and women of God who can give us so much, but we will miss them if we are only looking at the most visible people. Keep your heart and eyes open to receive the men and women God brings into your life. They may not be your senior pastor or an itinerant minister, but the fathers and mothers God has ordained for you will have what you need.

As you can tell from the people I listed and from the way I've been talking about fathers and mothers in the plural, I believe that we receive the benefits of covering from more than one person. Related to this is the truth that there are different levels of covering. For example, say that your life has been radically impacted by the teaching and ministry of Randy Clark, and for this reason you feel a connection with him. You can align yourself with Randy Clark even though you may never have a friendship with him. I can align myself under men like Billy Graham or even men who are no longer alive like John G. Lake. We can receive a download of wisdom and revelation from those we honor and listen to in the Body of Christ, and these things contribute to our spiritual covering.

However, there is another level of covering that only comes through having consistent personal contact with someone. You need more in your life than just a national leader with whom you have no chance of fostering a relationship. If I am to bring my life under covering, I need fathers and mothers in my life who have access to me and know what is going on with me on a consistent basis. I need a personal touch on most of the areas and issues in my life as I work through them.

Too many people think they have to make it on their own, and that anything they get from God they have to find solitarily. They have to fight their own battles. They have to obtain and master their own revelation. Now, I'm all for that. I fully realize that I am going to have to overcome struggles to gain ground, pursue my own encounters with God, and receive personal revelation. But I want to go further than those who have gone before me. I don't want to combat the same battles they have fought only to reach a similar place of revelation they have attained.

If revival is a structure God is building on the earth, then I don't want to spend my life building the same floor my fathers and mothers built. In other words, I can align my life under Bill Johnson's and step right into a revelation of healing that took him years to acquire. But when I do, I have a new responsibility. I must take what I received for free—paid for by another man—and steward it in such a way that it increases and more revelation is added. I must fight my own battles, not only to keep the revelation I was given, but also to steward it in such a way that it increases in my care. The spirit of independence has deceived us into thinking we need to strive on our own and learn things by ourselves, so we end up only reaching as far as those before us. Rather than working from the same floor in the building of revival that my fathers and mothers have built, I want to take what they've received and propel it to the next level. And that is what they want for me.

As I've mentioned, the Church's ability to sustain and increase revival from generation to generation has historically been limited because the generations were not properly connected. Except for a few isolated situations, revival has not carried on beyond one generation. Independence, disconnection, and improper alignment have robbed us of our spiritual inheritance. As an unfortunate result, though much of the revelation we live in now has been around for years, we have not built much higher upon it. If you read the sermons of men like John G. Lake, who lived in the early 1900s, you will see he was preaching the same things we currently are.[1] But I believe we are called to grasp what he learned and run even further in revelation and understanding. I believe this is happening and many in our day are faithfully stewarding the revelations given to past men and women of God and taking them even further. I can align myself under John G. Lake by honoring him, apprehending what he received and pressing in for more. If we are going to see revival sustained and passed from generation to generation, then we must understand the concept of inheritance. I aspire for Bill Johnson's ceiling to become my floor and for *my* sons and daughters to make my ceiling theirs.

I have found that the revelation of inheritance is affecting the way I pray. In the natural, if a son is working for his father in their family business and knows that one day it will be his, he thinks differently. The son wants his father to generate as much money as possible and to advance the business until it is as prosperous as it can become. As I came to understand inheritance and align myself as a son under Bill, I began to pray that Bill would access even more revelation than he currently had. As God downloads revelation into his life, I know it will be coming my way because I'm a spiritual son.

Certainly, I want my own revelation; I'm not just sitting around waiting for God to show Bill everything and then to glean it from him. But I love it when Bill receives new revelation because the principle of inheritance says that I partake of that revelation too. It's a family business, and I have aligned my heart under the covering of Bill.

Lou Engle's revelation on prayer, justice, Nazarite consecration, government, fasting—that's all mine. Danny Silk's inspiration on honor, relationships, leadership—that's all mine. Kris Vallotton's insight on the prophetic, church government, royalty—it's all mine. Cindy Jacob's instruction on taking nations, intercession, strategic thinking—all mine. Dann Farrelly's understanding of relational communication, grace, loyalty—I get it. I love it. I consider myself to be so blessed and honored to be aligned under the covering of spiritual fathers and mothers.

LEARNING TO SUBMIT

However, it wasn't always that way. I've had a bumpy road learning about covering and alignment. Walking out of Kris' office after the "you're independent" talk, I knew I needed to learn how to be a son and how to submit to covering, but I had no clue what I was facing in the journey ahead.

Some of the questions I found myself asking were: How do I think for myself but still allow fathers and mothers to speak into my life? How do I negotiate hearing from God while submitting my life to elders? What if I'm extremely passionate about something, but my covering doesn't think it's a good idea? What should I do then? What if I have a hard time connecting with them? In the end, I simply decided to make submission to my leaders a priority and apply it the best I could. My wife and I have both committed to learning this and we rarely, if ever, make a large decision without first submitting it to our fathers and mothers. Through experience, I now understand how safe it is to make decisions in a multitude of counselors (see Prov. 24:6).

Early on, however, I found it particularly difficult to concede to authority when I felt like I had a "God idea" and my leadership didn't agree. Now, I'm a rather passionate and opinionated guy. When I get an idea, I'm quite sure it will work and that it is from God. So it was hard when I submitted my plans to my covering and they had a different opinion. Proper alignment would be a breeze if my fathers and mothers agreed with everything I was doing and always said yes. But it didn't work like that. There were many meetings when I left frustrated because I had committed to remaining under covering, and their perception was at variance with mine. I thought, *It would be so much easier if I didn't have to move through this process. I wish I was the head guy and could just make the decision by myself.*

But again and again, as I submitted to authority, I discovered a whole new grace on my life. Things always seemed to work out, and at the end of the day I can genuinely say I have never once regretted submitting to my leaders. In fact, almost every time that I realized it was right to submit and did so, I avoided some kind of chaos, complication, or wrong diversion.

SERVING ANOTHER'S VISION

Another struggle I had coming under the covering of spiritual fathers and mothers was when it didn't feel like my plan was going as I had intended. Years ago, when I first started connecting to fathers and mothers, I had a concept of what connection would look like. I was young and envisioned there being numerous meetings where these men and women of God would sit with me for hours pouring out all the wisdom and revelation they had received. I imagined these different leaders recognizing the greatness in me and committing themselves to give their lives to see my destiny fulfilled. This is the part of the story where things didn't go as I expected. After about six months, I found myself getting frustrated because the fathers and mothers in my life were not pouring themselves out for me as much as I had envisioned.

In the midst of my frustration, I happened to go to dinner with Kris. I told Kris about my disappointment with this whole fathering thing and again, as Kris always does, he lovingly confronted me on my faulty mindset. He said, "Banning, you do well connecting with fathers when they are helping you seize your destiny and fulfill your vision. But when they don't do that, you become frustrated and want to leave. The problem with that attitude is that it's all about you. It's about *your* destiny and *your* vision. Can you serve your fathers even when it's not about you? Can you help them accomplish the things on their heart? Can you do everything in your power to see them step onto the stage of history and prioritize that over *you* stepping onto the stage of history?"

I hate it when Kris asks me questions like that. I had never thought of it in that way. Was I really frustrated with my connection with fathers because they weren't helping me reach my objective like I thought they should? Could I serve them and see their vision fulfilled even if it didn't further mine? Is this what it meant to be a son? Is this what the Lord was trying to teach me? If so, I thought, being a son was more difficult than I imagined.

Then I remembered the story of Elijah and Elisha. Elisha had committed to serve Elijah and to make sure that Elijah had what he needed. Elisha was not concerned about his own ministry or his destiny; he was attentive to Elijah and making sure he was successful. Second Kings chapter 2 recounts the story of Elisha following Elijah right before the Lord took Elijah to Heaven. Three times during the journey, Elijah turned to Elisha and told him to stay behind because the Lord was going to take him. But each time, Elisha refused to leave even though he knew that Elijah's time had come. Many Bible scholars believe that at each city where Elijah told him to stay, Elisha had the opportunity to begin his own ministry by taking over a school of the prophets. But Elisha declined each opportunity to develop his own ministry and stayed with Elijah to serve him until the end. To Elisha, it wasn't about his up-and-coming worldwide ministry; it was about serving his spiritual father. Elisha also knew that Elijah had what he needed—the mantle—and he needed to be successful in serving to secure it.

In the restaurant with Kris, I once again shifted the way I thought and decided that even if my fathers and mothers didn't help me get to my destiny, I was going to serve them and do everything I could to see them enter further into their destiny. It turned out that learning to serve my fathers and mothers as a son even when I didn't see how it would help me get to where I was going was actually a key part of God's plan. Although I couldn't see how it worked, God was moving me forward in my destiny. This is how God set it up to work—as soon as I purposed to serve my spiritual fathers' vision, I was being propelled toward mine. Even though it looked different than I first imagined, I am forever indebted to the fathers and mothers for what they have sown into my life.

Over the years, people have come up to me and asked what they should do if they don't have any vision for their life. I respond with the truth I have learned in serving my fathers and mothers: "Serve someone else's vision." Jesus asked us, *"And if you have not been faithful in what is another man's, who will give you what is your own?"* (Luke 16:12). Catching this principle is crucial to understanding covering. Jesus will release to us the things we have been faithful with in someone else's life. If you want your own anointing, serve someone else's anointing. If you want vision, be a great steward to someone else's vision. If you want your own ministry, attend to someone else's ministry. If you want to walk in healing, assist someone who moves in healing.

Moses understood this principle. Exodus 3 tells of Moses encountering God at the burning bush and receiving his commission to lead the people of Israel out of captivity. One day as I read that passage, a phrase jumped out at me in verse 1: *"Now Moses was tending the flock of Jethro his father-in-law…"* (Exod. 3:1). I sat thinking about that for a while and then realized why the Lord had slipped in a seemingly insignificant line like that. Moses received his ministry of shepherding the people of Israel in the context of his faithfulness with another man's flock. One of the greatest leaders in the Bible spent 40 years on the backside of a desert shepherding someone else's sheep! I speculate it was hard, confusing, and frustrating at times. I'm certain that deep inside, Moses knew he was destined for more than shepherding. He had a sense of the call of God on his life and knew that God was going to do great things through him. Thankfully, for the people of Israel, Moses learned how to be loyal in the desert. Moses first had to be trustworthy and dependable with his father-in-law's sheep before he was given his own.

The hard part about serving another's vision is that it's not about you. You have to put your vision aside and truly serve another's if the Lord is going to give you what is your own. I talk to people all the time and ask them, "Who are you serving on purpose?" Many people can't answer that question. Some are involved in different types of ministry, but it's still all about them. Someone might be a drummer on the worship team, for example, except their motivation in serving is to improve as a drummer, not to be faithful to the vision of the worship leader. You can always tell what is motivating a person to serve when he or she doesn't get to do what he or she wants. What happens when that drummer isn't utilized to play on a consistent basis? If his heart is to be faithful with the vision of the worship leader, then it won't matter where he assists in that ministry. This is where the rubber meets the road. To truly serve someone else is an act of humility. But the Bible says that if you humble yourself, God will exalt you in due time (see 1 Pet. 5:6). You will be released into your ministry and vision when the timing is right.

GETTING INTO THE FLOW OF GRACE

I have heard it said that grace is "God's empowerment to do what we are called to do." What a great description. When grace is in your life, there is a power to do what's on your heart. Whether it's writing books, preaching, running a business, or living a life of holiness, it's grace that makes it possible. When I am properly aligned under the leaders God has placed in my life, grace flows freely in my life. This principle is pictured in Psalm 133:1-2:

> Behold, how good and how pleasant it is for brethren to dwell together in unity! It is like the precious oil upon the head, running down on the beard, the beard of Aaron, running down on the edge of his garments.

Unity speaks of proper alignment, and oil speaks of the anointing of the Holy Spirit—of grace. When I aligned myself under spiritual authority, a level of grace began to flow in my life that I had never before experienced, because the oil that was flowing from the head started to run all over me. I felt a wind pushing me forward that I had never sensed before. I remind you again of First Peter 5:5, which says: *"Likewise you younger people, submit yourselves to your elders. Yes, all of you be submissive to one another, and be clothed with humility, for 'God resists the proud, but gives **grace** to the humble.'"* There's a grace that comes from being under covering.

I used to love Slip 'n Slides as a kid. Recently we bought our kids their first Slip 'n Slide. What a blast! But this one was way cooler than any I had played on as a kid. It had two slides side-by-side for two children to race each other. A perfect arch of water squirted out from the middle to cover the ride which ended in a small pool of water backed by an inflatable cushion. This Slip 'n Slide was high tech! My wife and I just laughed and laughed as we delighted in our three kids scooting down in glee—over and over. It looked like so much fun that the two of us were wondering if people in their thirties could still negotiate the Slip 'n Slide.

Slip 'n Slides are a blast, that is, when they have water on them. Without H_2O, they are a completely different experience—not fun. Imagine running at full speed, launching forward into a perfect horizontal position in the air, and landing on a Slip 'n Slide with no water. Ouch! Living life without grace is like diving onto a Slip 'n Slide with no water. I see many people who, because they aren't under covering, are trying to live life without grace. They always feel like there is a wind resisting them as they attempt to move forward. They feel as if they were meant to fly but can never get off the ground.

There are people who sit in my office and tell me that the devil is resisting them and they can't figure out why. But sometimes it's not the devil hindering them; it's God resisting them. They have refused to submit their lives to covering as is commanded in First Peter, so God is resisting the pride in them. I heard Rick Joyner once say, "I would rather have a thousand demons resisting me than God resisting me." I agree! It's not a good idea to have God hinder you. Yet I've seen firsthand that when someone harnesses the revelation of covering and submits to spiritual authority, the wind shifts in that person's life. Instead of resistance, he feels the wind accelerating him toward his destiny.

Gen-14 is a hip-hop ministry based out of Bethel Church. They are an incredible group whose heart is not only to produce great hip-hop music but also to minister freedom to a generation. They don't just have concerts; they have full-blown revival meetings at their concerts with signs and wonders, deliverances, and salvations. Years ago, they were struggling to mobilize things, and the dreams in their hearts were not getting off the ground. They were confused as to why they weren't seeing the impact and momentum they knew they were called to see.

Rich Potillor, one of the group members, told me at lunch one day about their frustration. I talked to him briefly about the need to be aligned under covering and the benefits that come with it. They had been attending Bethel for a while, but had never officially sat down with any of the leaders and brought their ministry to them. Rich knew that's what they were supposed to do and immediately set up meetings with a handful of the pastors. They began to receive input within a covering they had not had before. Almost instantly, the wind in their ministry shifted and they began to see a new level of grace come on them. It was so encouraging to watch these men and women of God from Gen-14 begin to step fully into their destiny as part of the new breed emerging in the earth.

COURAGE

I want to describe some of the benefits that come to your life through covering. The first is courage. Billy Graham said, "Courage is contagious. When a brave man takes a stand, the spines of others are stiffened."[2] God is calling a generation to live courageously. I have the privilege of ministering to youth and young adults all over the world, and it is clear to me that what they need is courage. God is calling this new breed of revivalists to great things. He is calling them to change the world, to do the impossible, to see campuses rocked, cities taken, and nations shifted. All of that requires a tremendous amount of courage. They will never be able to do what is on their hearts or see revival without boldness. It takes courage to follow Jesus and be a world-changer, and one of the primary ways courage comes is through the affirmation and modeling of fathers and mothers.

Esther needed courage to change the world and do what she was called to do in her day. God had set Esther apart to save her people, so He connected her with Mordecai, a cousin who took her in when her parents died. He became her father. Mordecai knew Esther must stand before the king if her people were going to survive the plot of Haman to destroy them. But fulfilling that task wasn't easy. In those days, people did not just walk in on the king without an invitation, because they could be killed, unless the king wanted to receive them and extended his scepter. When Mordecai told Esther she must go before the king for her people, her response revealed the struggle within her to be courageous:

> *All the king's servants and the people of the king's prov-*
> *inces know that any man or woman who goes into the*
> *inner court to the king, who has not been called, he has*

but one law: put all to death, except the one to whom the king holds out the golden scepter, that he may live. Yet I myself have not been called to go in to the king these thirty days (Esther 4:11).

Esther did not want to go before the king because she knew it might cost her her life. In the end she made the decision to risk her life, declaring, *"If I perish, I perish"* (Esther 4:16). I've heard many preachers call us to have the courage of Esther, to be those who would *"...love not their lives unto the death"* (Rev. 12:11 KJV). But Esther did not have the fortitude necessary to do what she was called to without Mordecai. It was her spiritual father who modeled courage and encouraged and strengthened her to move ahead no matter what the cost:

And Mordecai told them to answer Esther: "Do not think in your heart that you will escape in the king's palace any more than all the other Jews. For if you remain completely silent at this time, relief and deliverance will arise for the Jews from another place, but you and your father's house will perish. Yet who knows whether you have come to the kingdom for such a time as this?" (Esther 4:13-14)

It was because of Mordecai's input in her life that Esther received the courage necessary to fulfill her destiny—a courage she had previously lacked. As a result, a nation was saved because of Esther's alignment under Mordecai.

WISDOM

I have a conviction that I always need to be in over my head in ministry. If I am approaching a place where I feel comfortable or that I know what I'm doing, I need to find a deeper pool and plunge in. It's how I prefer to live, and it means I am constantly required to stretch and grow as a leader. However, the only reason this has worked for me is because of my connection with fathers and mothers. As long as

I am yoked with them, I know that in any situation I will have access to the wisdom and guidance necessary to be successful.

I mentioned my time as a leader in Bethel School of Supernatural Ministry. I was 25 and in way over my head, but I had an immense value for fathers and was closely linked to them as I led four incredible classes of revivalists. I remember being in a counseling session with a student where I had no idea what to do. I asked the person to hold on one second. I rushed downstairs, interrupted a meeting Danny Silk was having, and asked him what I should do. He advised me, so then I was able to walk confidently back upstairs into the counseling session and say, "All right, here's some ideas."

I can't begin to tell you how many hours I spent in Dann Farrelly's office pulling as much wisdom as I could get out of him. If you have a value for fathers and mothers, you will be able to go further than you ever thought possible. I cannot imagine having to live life relying solely on the level of wisdom and experience I have. Through relationship, I have access to the discernment and foresight of men and women who are years ahead of me.

God is raising up a people in the earth who will display the wisdom of God. The Book of Proverbs is filled with encouragement to pursue and value wisdom, and very significantly these exhortations were given to a son by his father. Young revivalists must be connected to fathers and mothers in order to receive greater understanding. Joshua was a leader who walked in wisdom, and Deuteronomy 34:9 explains that Joshua was full of the spirit of wisdom because Moses had laid his hands on him. Joshua received wisdom because of his joining to Moses. Esther likewise received from Mordecai wisdom that made her successful.

One of the main ways this inheritance of wisdom shows up is in the ability to learn from the mistakes and successes of our fathers and mothers. I see no reason why my children need to make the same mistakes I made to learn the same things I mastered. If they can connect with me, they can gain the things I assimilated without having to go through the same process. They will have to learn from their own mistakes, but those errors should teach them new things.

It has been a huge honor and an amazing experience to serve under Bill Johnson. He approaches life from such a unique perspective, and it works well. His approach to ministry, family, healing, the Kingdom, and his relationship with God just works so effectively.

One day I asked him, "How did you figure out how to do the things you are doing that seem to work so well?"

Without hesitation, he answered, "Because I've tried a lot of things that didn't work."

Wow! Why would I try all the things Bill has tried only to find out what doesn't work? I can unite my life with his and learn the things that do not work and the things that do work. I don't have time to waste trying to figure out everything on my own. I want to learn from my fathers and mothers. There will be some things I have to ascertain on my own, but I want to amass as much as I can from the older generation.

PROTECTION

A youth pastor friend of mine told me a great story. When he was around eight years old, he made a frog hotel. It was really just a muddy crater in the ground, but he loved it. He would plunk their frogs in there and spend hours playing in the mud. One afternoon, my friend walked out of his house just in time to see his older brother throwing darts at his favorite frog. Screaming at the top of his lungs, he rushed to protect his favorite frog and stuck his hand out as a shield. Yep, you guessed it! As he did, his brother flung one more dart. But the dart never struck the frog because it pierced the outstretched hand of my friend. He was crying and hollering with a dart protruding from his hand, but his beloved frog was saved.

It is amazing how many people I meet who are getting thrashed in life because they have no covering. The spirit of independence has separated them from covering and community, and darts are striking and hurting them. It's not really that complicated. If it's raining and you don't wish to get soaked, then jump under an umbrella.

However, it is common sense that if you step outside the shelter, you will find yourself wet. In my own life as a young man, I had fathers and mothers who protected me. The darts of the enemy didn't have easy access in my life. I had to fight my own battles and learn how to be victorious, but it was much easier under covering.

IDENTITY

My full name is Banning Wesley Liebscher. For years I thought I knew the definition of my first and last names. In sixth grade, a mother at the Christian school I attended volunteered to find out what each of our first names meant. She came back and gave each of us a little certificate that announced these meanings to the world. My name's description was "Strong Warrior, Great Protector." Of course, as a young boy I was stoked to find out that my name had such a powerful meaning. And I not only had a great first name; my last name was also powerful. My parents always told me that my last name meant "lover." It's a German name—*lieb* means "love," so we always thought our last name meant "lover." What a cool name I had—"Strong Warrior, Great Protector, Lover." It doesn't get much better than that.

A few years after I got married, SeaJay and I were in a bookstore and we found my name in a baby book. I had never seen my name in a baby book and was excited to have proof of the greatness that my name proclaimed about my life. But when I read the meaning of my name, which was Irish, my world began to crumble around me. It didn't say "Strong Warrior, Great Protector." It actually meant, "Small, Fair One." *Small, Fair One!* I couldn't believe it. I was crushed. I pulled myself together and reassured myself that at least I still had a cool last name. But that changed a few months later when a man from Germany visited our church.

My friend was talking to him and mentioned that my last name was German and meant "lover." "Liebscher?" he responded with a quizzical look. "Liebscher doesn't mean 'lover.'"

My friend couldn't believe it. "Well then, what does it mean?"

The German paused for a moment and then said, "I think it means 'love handles.'"

When my friend told me this, it was just too much. In a matter of months I had gone from "Strong Warrior, Great Protector, Lover," to "Small, Fair One, Love Handles." Because of this, I've made certain all three of my children have powerfully prophetic names. My oldest is called to be a prophetess to the nations. My middle child is called to be an evangelist who is poured out for an end-time harvest. And my youngest is called to be an apostolic healer. Each of their names is directly connected to their identity and calling in God.

Names don't mean too much in our society, but in biblical times what one called a child was a big deal. It was a prophetic declaration over his or her life. It helped to define that person and impart identity. Many young revivalists lack identity because their spiritual fathers and mothers have never named them. It's the role of parents to "describe" a child through their choice of name. A child doesn't decide his or her name; the *parents* do. There is something powerful that happens when you align yourself under a Moses, an Elijah, or a Mordecai and they begin to call out the greatness in your life. As they decree prophetically who you are, you begin to establish your identity in God.

Knowing who you are in God produces security, and that security produces confidence. I remember once being at a local high school basketball game. There were 1,500 people jammed into that gymnasium, most of them teenagers. You could feel the insecurity in the room; it was almost tangible. I looked at the generation I was called to father and I knew if I could give them anything it would be confidence. As they wade into a world fluctuating with self-doubt, peer pressure, and the unknown, what they need is confidence—a resolution to stand firm and not waver no matter how intense the storm, and a sureness to stand up for Jesus even if it costs them their reputation.

The generational disconnect has cut off the ability of the younger generation to find out who they are so they can walk in the level of self-possession and daring God has intended for them. When you are firmly established in who you are, confidence begins to burst forth in your life. God has given fathers and mothers the privilege of spiritually naming sons and daughters, and I intend to be one who does this for those He entrusts to me.

OUR CHOICES

There are two choices in front of us. These are the same two options found in the rest of Second Kings 2. After Elijah was taken to Heaven in a whirlwind, Elisha, who had diligently followed and served Elijah until the end, received his mantle and a double portion. Immediately, Elisha stepped into an incredible anointing to perform signs and wonders. We find evidence that he was properly aligned with Elijah in his second miracle, which was healing the water source of an entire community. But the same chapter records an event that has always confused me. A group of youths began to mock Elisha, and as they jeered, two female bears came out of the woods and mauled 42 of them. Why would that story be in the Bible? Sometimes when I read the Bible I think it is so random. But I believe that the Lord is trying to show us our two alternatives. We can, like Elisha, properly align ourselves under spiritual authority by honoring and serving them and receive an inheritance of courage, wisdom, identity, protection, and anointing for signs and wonders, or we can detach ourselves through dishonoring them and be destroyed. The choice is ours.

HEARTS OF THE FATHERS

As I have said, most of my ministry over the years has been targeted toward youth and young adults—those in their teens and twenties. Because of that, the majority of my teaching on the subject of covering and alignment has been on young people honoring the older generation. But there is more to this principle in Scripture than just the hearts of the children turning to their fathers (see Mal. 4:6). As I mentioned before, Malachi first mentions the *"hearts of the fathers"* turning to the children, and then the hearts of the children turning to the fathers. Honor must flow in both directions. The older generation must take their place in covering the younger generation, and this covering must extend from a heart of love and honor.

As I've stated throughout this chapter, I believe with all of my heart that the younger generation desperately needs the older generation. But I also believe the older generation desperately needs the younger generation. Like a team competing to win a relay race, we must understand how to hand off the baton. It's not enough for each runner to be fast. If the members of the relay team only practice getting quicker but never rehearse handing off the baton, the race will be lost. What a shame for a generation to experience revival and a great outpouring of the Holy Spirit, but not know how to pass on the baton successfully so the generations to come can finish the race.

We see this principle authenticated in the lives of Elijah, Elisha, and Gehazi. (See First and Second Kings.) Elijah had a dream to see the reign of Jezebel end and the people of Israel restored to the one true God. But Elijah never saw that happen in his lifetime. He tasted some victories, but he never witnessed the reign of Jezebel come to an end. However, Elijah knew how to pass the baton to the next generation. Succeeding Elijah were Elisha and Jehu. These two spiritual sons of Elijah saw what he had dreamed of—the government of Jezebel dismantled in their day. Elisha needed Elijah to receive a double-portion anointing, but Elijah needed Elisha to see his dream fulfilled.

Unfortunately, though, the story doesn't end well. Elisha was training Gehazi and I believe was going to pass the baton off to him. But because of Gehazi's disobedience and greed, the baton was dropped and the anointing that had started with Elijah, and had been passed on to Elisha with increased power, was ended after only two generations. Can you imagine what would have happened if Gehazi had been faithful? I believe he would have had the same opportunity Elisha had to gain access to a double portion of the anointing on his father. If he had received a double portion of Elisha's anointing, which was a double portion of Elijah's, then Gehazi could have walked in an anointing four times greater than that of Elijah. That is my vision—to see the generations walking together in proper alignment, and the baton of revival successfully passing and increasing from one generation to the next—until the return of Christ.

I want to end with a story that poignantly represents what the heart of God is for this hour. I read this in an article years ago in college. I'm not sure who wrote it, but I remember I liked it so much that I copied it down:

> Rosenbury was riding in a train on his way to a speaking engagement. He noticed a boy in his late teens acting very nervous, moving from one seat to another. Dr. Rosenbury approached the boy and asked him if he could be of some help. The boy told his story. "I used to live in Springvale just a few miles ahead. This train goes right behind our back yard. My father and mother still live in the old house. Three years ago I had a fight with my dad and ran away from home. It has been three tough years. I wrote my mom last week and told her I wanted to come home just once and if dad agreed she was going to hang something white outside the house so I would know that my father had agreed to let me stop. I told her not to do it unless father had agreed to let me come home." Dr. Rosenbury noticed the boy becoming increasingly agitated as he said, "Look sir, my house is just a few miles ahead and I am afraid to look. I am going to close my eyes. Would you look and see if you can see anything white hanging in the yard?" As the train came around the corner Rosenbury shouted, "Look, son, look!" You could hardly see the house for white. There was a large sheet hanging from the upstairs window, tablecloths, hankies, pillowcases hung on every tree, all across the clothes line, hanging from every window. The boy's face went white, his lips quivered as the train came

to a stop. Rosenbury says that the last thing he saw of the boy he was running as fast as he could to the house of his father.

It is time for the sons and daughters to come home to their mothers and fathers. God is joining the generations in proper alignment, bringing the rod and the sword together for worldwide revival. He truly is turning *"the hearts of the fathers to the children, and the hearts of the children to their fathers"* (Mal. 4:6).

SECTION III

THE BURNING ONES

THIS NEW BREED of revivalist is passionately in love with God and is being awakened to His extravagant love for them. They are allowing their blazing desire for Him to infuse all that they are and all that they do. Known as Burning Ones, their lives ignite revival fires across the world.

It is not only possible for you and me to live a life of sustained passionate love, but it is achievable to live a life escalating in passion, to abide continually in the Lord's extreme love.

Lovers are distinguishable because they are not motivated by accolades or money, but by a deep love for Jesus (or their King). This compels them to make radical choices marked by sacrifice, risk, humility, and excellence. They have found their significance in their relationship with the Lord and understand their value. They are secure in their identity and embrace God's deep purposes for them. They display God's goodness, greatness, and glory in and through their lives, and boldly welcome the world to experience God for themselves.

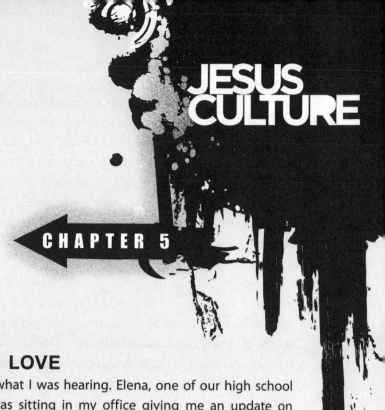

JESUS CULTURE

CHAPTER 5

AWAKENED LOVE

I couldn't believe what I was hearing. Elena, one of our high school campus leaders, was sitting in my office giving me an update on the campus ministry we had just launched. Her job was to activate Christian students to pray on her campus, and our strategy was simple: She was to gather other Christian students on her campus and challenge them to pray for five of their unsaved friends. Our goal was to see every unsaved student on the campus prayed for by name every week. Elena had connected with a handful of other Christian students and started organizing weekly prayer times. But a few weeks later, her Christian friends approached her and said that they were no longer interested in praying anymore and weren't going to attend the weekly prayer meetings.

When she told me this, I was stunned. As I thought about it, I realized that it seemed so *unnatural* for Christian young people—or any Christians, for that matter—not to be passionate about the things of God. More specifically, it is abnormal for Christians not to be passionately in love with God and, in turn, enamored with the things of God. In fact, passionate love should be the substance that primarily characterizes us as believers. Unfortunately, much of the Church has promoted the idea that the hallmark of the believer's life is his or her ability to observe certain spiritual disciplines—to go to church regularly, to read the Bible, and to avoid doing bad things. But as Bill Johnson says, "Christianity was never meant to be a life of disciplines. It was always meant to be a life of passion." The most natural thing in the Christian life is to be passionately in love with Jesus and for this blazing love to infuse all that we are and do. In fact, as human beings we were created to live passionately and are drawn to those who live with fervor.

I remember once being glued to my television for an hour watching Steve Irwin, one of the most animated and intense people who have lived on the face of the planet. Irwin had a popular educational television show, *The Crocodile Hunter*, which explored the world of reptiles and other wildlife. In this particular episode of *The Crocodile Hunter,* Irwin went on a search for the ten most venomous land snakes in the world. The most venomous land snake is found on the continent of Australia. After two difficult days of traveling into the Outback, Irwin finally located the snake he had been searching for.

Now, this is not a reptile most people want to find. The venom in a single bite has enough potency to kill a thousand men. However, the insanely enthusiastic Irwin lay quietly on his stomach just feet away from it! I sat there in my living room in disbelief as the most deadly land snake in the world slowly slithered up to Irwin, who calmly allowed it to lick his face. I was ready to jump out of my skin in fear, but not Steve. As the snake casually slithered away, he jumped up and acted like someone just told him he had won a million dollars.

I don't care at all about snakes, but I couldn't pull away from watching the passion of Steve Irwin. And I'm convinced that most other fans of *The Crocodile Hunter* weren't necessarily extremely interested in crocodiles or snakes, but were likewise fascinated by a man who lived with so much energetic conviction. Many people who don't live with passion live vicariously through movies, sports, or the experiences of others. We love to follow Olympic athletes who are willing to sacrifice years of their lives in training because of their determination to be the best in the world at something. And most of us enjoy movies about romance, loyalty, and courage because they tap into something deep within us that knows we were born to live wholeheartedly.

Olympic athletes and characters like Steve Irwin show us that passionate people make sacrifices and take risks. I believe we are attracted to passion because there is something within us that knows we were meant to give our lives for something greater than ourselves, and passionate love is really the only force strong enough to drive us beyond convenience and into sacrifice. Discipline will never be enough.

Most of us don't really associate the word "discipline" with risk-taking. Now, I am a firm believer in disciplines and encourage Christians to embrace them, but they can never be the propulsive stimulus in our lives. The reason for this is that the greater thing we were made for—the thing we were meant to give our lives for—is *relationship*, first with God, and then with one another. And passion is the only driving force that makes sense in relationships.

My marriage with my wife is not a marriage of disciplines. Although it would be untrue to say that every day of marriage is bursting with passionate love, I am married to my wife because I am fervently in love with her, not because I am in a business contract with her. It is true that love is a choice, not just a feeling I have, but I don't wake up every day saying, "Today, I am going to choose to love my wife." My passion for my wife is what drives me as I walk out my promise to spend the rest of my life with her.

I understand that many times we do the right thing in our relationship with God simply because we know it's the correct thing to do. It is absolutely necessary to pray, worship, spend time with God, and read your Bible because it is the right thing to do. But doing the right thing is not the ultimate goal, and our relationship with God cannot be based solely on being "correct" out of discipline. God cares about more than our doing the right thing. The right thing is just that—the right thing. This is because it is connected to our ultimate purpose, which is loving Him and being loved by Him. God's paramount goal for each of us is a heart awakened with love for Jesus that yields a life willing to sacrifice everything, and it can only happen through passion. Impassioned love is the fuel we were made to burn. Disciplines are like guardrails on the highway. They help to buffer us so that we remain on the road. But they will never really be substantial enough to keep our engine running.

CALLED TO SUSTAINED PASSION

As my team of leaders and I began to train and commission youth and young adults, I came face to face with the reality that many Christian young people were not living passionately for God or the things of God. They may have experienced them from time to time at camps or conferences, and most of them had the desire to live passionately, but they were not sure how to sustain that type of lifestyle. It's one thing to experience moments of rapture for God, but it's an entirely different thing to live a *life* of passion.

One of our primary strategies for leading young people into a life of passion has been simply to call out the hunger that is already inside them. Bill Johnson taught me early in my ministry to preach to all people as if they were hungry for the things of God. He himself preaches with the assumption that people have an appetite for God, because if they are Christians they have the Holy Spirit inside of them, who is affectionate for and inclined toward God. If they're not Christians, they have a longing for God as well because they were made for Him. Bill likes to point out that this is why Jesus is called the *"Desire of All Nations"* (see Hag. 2:7). He is the perfect fulfillment to the deepest yearnings of the human heart.

I believe that young people are genuinely hungry to live passionately for God, but that ache has been buried and needs to be called out. As my team and I have worked to call out this craving, we have not only seen hearts awakening with zeal for God, we have also seen young people discovering that it is possible to live a life of sustained passion. In fact, it is not only possible to sustain passion, it is also achievable to live a life that escalates in passion year after year. The new revivalists emerging in the earth are experiencing the long burn of love, not just the short burst of an experience that quickly fades away.

One of the primary keys to sustaining an increasing passion for God is found in the Book of Revelation. The apostle John, while in exile on the Island of Patmos, was taken to Heaven and came face to face with Jesus. In this encounter, Jesus gave John certain messages to write to various churches. The message He delivered to the church in Ephesus was that He saw the good works they were doing, but that He had one thing against them: *"Nevertheless I have this against you, that you have left your first love. Remember therefore from where you have fallen; repent and do the first works…"* (Rev. 2:4-5). I grew up in the church and have heard this passage of Scripture taught many times. The message always went something like this: "When you are first saved, you are naturally on fire for God and live life full of passion. You love to pray, read your Bible, invite people to church, and witness. But eventually, as your journey takes you further down the road of the Christian life, your fire and passion for God begin to diminish." In conclusion, we were always encouraged to return to our "first love" by remembering how we used to live as new Christians and becoming like that once again.

Remember, deep inside every Christian is a desire to live thoroughly in love with Jesus. Those of us who heard this message wanted more passion in our lives and responded by working hard to get back to where we used to be in our early Christian life. We tried to do the same things we used to, but since we were performing them from duty rather than passion, it rarely produced the same results and the attempt was always short-lived.

The problem with this teaching is the conclusion that going back to our first love means going back to how we first loved Jesus. I don't think that is what Revelation 2 is talking about. First John says, *"We love Him because He **first loved** us"* (1 John 4:19). I don't believe Jesus was telling us to return to how we first loved Him; I am convinced

He was telling us to return to the revelation that He first loved us. *It's the revelation of His love for us that awakens our love for Him.* When you encounter His all-consuming love for you, the natural response is to be completely in love with Him. His love incites ours to the point where we don't have to strive or struggle to live a life of passion. It just comes naturally.

In my office, sitting on my bookshelf, is a Winnie the Pooh doll. It is a reminder to me of something the Lord showed me years ago. For my daughter's first Easter, my wife and I bought her this stuffed animal. It is a great toy and far more technologically advanced than anything I had as a kid. This Winnie the Pooh character holds a baby rattle and came with a larger rattle for my daughter to play with. Whenever she waved the large rattle in front of Winnie the Pooh, the small rattle in Pooh's hand picked up a signal and he began to dance and sing, "I am short and fat and proud of that and so with all my might I up-down, up-down…." And whenever my daughter stopped waving the rattle, Winnie the Pooh immediately ceased dancing and singing.

The stuffed toy on my shelf regularly reminds me that when God's "rattle" is active in my life, then I come alive. I'm sure you get the picture. Our love for God is awakened when we encounter His love for us. It is only when we are consistently experiencing God's intense love for us that we have the ability to live a life of fiery love for Him. Mike Bickle says, "We need God to love God."[2] We truly can do nothing apart from Him.

Jesus taught this truth to His disciples when He said, *"As the Father loved Me, I also have loved you; abide in My love"* (John 15:9). What a staggering statement. Jesus said that He loves us the same way God the Father loves Him. There isn't a greater love than that. He then called us to *abide* in that love. He didn't tell us to try to recreate the love we used to have when we first got saved and then abide in *our love for Him*, but to learn to abide in *His love for us*. He was saying, in essence, "My love for you is so extravagant. Your 'first works' are to learn to live a life connected to My exorbitant love." Every day we get the opportunity to abide in the most extreme, zealous, over-the-top, wild, mind-blowing love imaginable. When we learn to do that, the natural response will always be extravagant love for Him.

The new breed of revivalist that is emerging in the earth is learning the secret of abiding in the love of Jesus, and thus they are burning with passion for Him. Their hearts are molten—liquefied by His unquenchable love—and they are being poured out upon others. They will be known as Burning Ones, whose lives ignite revival fires across the globe. Because they walk in the revelation of friendship with God, they do not work *for* Him but *with* Him. They are *lovers* of God, not *employees* of God. The lives of lovers stand out because they are not motivated by fame or fortune but by a deep love for Jesus. Their passion compels them to go beyond the status quo, and therefore their lives are marked by sacrifice, risk, humility, and excellence. Mike Bickle says, "Lovers always get more work done than workers."[3]

If we are to live as Burning Ones, we must encounter the All-Consuming Fire. One of our young people had a dream the first year we went to England with Jesus Culture. In the dream there was a Man standing in a field with a propane bottle nozzle sticking out of His neck. A group of young people gathered around Him, but soon realized He was about to burst into flames and quickly retreated to a safe distance. However, they were very intrigued by this Man and lingered to watch him. He began to call them to come close. One by one, the young people drew closer to the Man in the field. All of a sudden, they heard "Tick, Tick, Tick, Tick," and He burst into flames, consuming them all. Jesus is calling us to draw close so that He can ignite us with the fire of His love, and this new breed is responding to that call.

As we see in this dream, there is a progression of invitation, pursuit, and encounter in our relationship with God. If we are going to abide in the love of God, this advancement must be cyclical in our lives. In my own life it happens something like this: My heart responds to God's invitation and I encounter His amazing love for me. That experience with His love sparks a love within me that says, "Lord, You are all I want. *You* are the one I've been looking for. I will spend my entire life in pursuit of You." That pursuit gets me back into His presence, where I encounter more of His love, which ignites another level of passion in my life for Jesus, causing me to want to pursue Him even more. As long as this sequence is nurtured, so is the heightening of my passion.

I think back to the times in my life where the Lord revealed His love to me in fresh ways. My natural response was always to grow more in adulation and tenderness for Him. I remember one morning in particular when I slipped into our sanctuary. The lights were out, no chairs were set up, and I lay down by the stage to pray. As I prayed, I was overwhelmed with the love of God. It was tangible. I could feel waves of love flowing over me. I lay there just weeping as I experienced again the love of God. After that experience, my heart was flaming with love for Him. But it's important to see that the nature of the cycle reveals that, as I said before, our pursuit of the Lord is dependent on Him in at least two ways. Firstly, it is dependent on God in that our pursuit of Him can really only ever be a *response* to His courting of us. As Jesus declared, *"No one can come to Me unless the Father who sent Me draws him"* (John 6:44). My searching out God happened because I had a revelation that He was in pursuit of me. Revelation 3:20 says, *"Behold I stand at the door and knock."* Jesus is the One standing at the door knocking. We didn't find Jesus; He found us. He wasn't lost; we were lost. More importantly, God's quest in capturing your heart doesn't stop when you become saved. He is still in pursuit of you, even today!

Similarly, I worked hard at attracting my wife when we were dating. I wanted her to say yes when I asked her to marry me. But I didn't stop pursuing her when we said our vows. Eleven years later I am still in pursuit of capturing her heart. God is still pursuing us just as intensely as before we were saved. Every day His heart longs to be with you, and He is coming after you. I often tell people, "It's not hard to find God. You just have to stop long enough for Him to find you."

When you stay still long enough for Him to find you and you drink of His love like I have described, something awakens inside. This is the other way in which our following eagerly after God is dependent on Him. Encountering the Lord's love for us not only gives us something to respond to, it enables us to reciprocate. The experience actually imparts something you didn't have before—that awakened heart of passion that drives you in your pursuit.

REVELATION BEYOND INFORMATION

The apostle Paul prayed that we would *"know the love of Christ which passes knowledge..."* (Eph. 3:19). The verse concludes: *"that you may be filled up to all the fullness of God."* Experience is the key to fullness because it brings *revelation*. Without the revelation knowledge that comes by experience, we are limited to operating with only *information*. Most Christians have the correct information. In the majority of churches, if I were to ask, "Do you believe Jesus loves you?" I'm certain that 99 percent of the congregation would respond with a sincere *yes*. The mere fact that you are reading this book tells me that you probably believe Jesus loves you. But are you responding out of information or revelation?

When Evander Holyfield, the former heavyweight boxing champion, was in his prime, I loved to watch his fights. After seeing just a few of his fights, it became obvious to me that *he hits hard*. My observation was reinforced as I read the articles about his fights, listened to commentators talk about his boxing style, and heard other fighters being interviewed about their experiences with Holyfield in the ring. If you were to ask me, "Does Evander Holyfield punch hard?" I would say with conviction, "Yes. Evander Holyfield hits hard." But as strong and true an answer as that is, it is completely based in the realm of information. It doesn't actually become a *personal revelation* until I lace up the boxing shoes, slip on the boxing gloves, and step into the ring with Holyfield himself. About five seconds into the first round, when Holyfield's fist connects with my jaw and my knees buckle and little birdies begin to circle around my head, it's in *that* moment that revelation impacts me: "Evander Holyfield hits hard!" It's the exact same response as I would have given before, but now it's *revelation*—not purely information. I wouldn't only have read about how hard he punches; I would have experienced it for myself!

Too many people are content to live a life of information rather than revelation. But knowledge alone will never inflame a sustained blaze in you to love Jesus passionately. Only revelation will do that. Remember, Ephesians 3:19 says that the revelation that comes by experience is the key to *fullness*. That Greek word translated "fullness" refers to a ship that is filled with merchandise and sailors. A ship can be seaworthy and a destination decided and underway, but if you don't have the cargo on board or the manpower to sail the ship you are not going anywhere. The same is true for us if we only have information without revelation and the reality of experience that brings God's fullness into our lives.

The revelation of His extravagant love will propel you deeper into God's heart because you will long to be with Him. E.M. Bounds, talking about those who have encountered the Father's love, says, "They spend much time in prayer, not because they watch the shadow on the dial or the hands on the clock, but because it is to them so momentous and engaging a business that they can scarcely quit."[4]

THE POWER OF YES

It seems so easy, doesn't it? All we have to do is abide in His love and our passion for God will be ignited. And may I remind you that getting a revelation of God's love is not difficult. It really is mostly a matter of slowing down and positioning yourself to receive from Him. As much as you long to experience God's love for you, He wants it far more. But while God's love is always available, we live in a society that wars against our pursuit of it. Never in all of history have there been so many distractions available to us. No other generation has been inundated with hundreds of television stations, text messaging, e-mails, Internet, cell phones, mobile video games, digital music players that hold thousands of songs, movies on demand, and the ability to travel. While those distractions are not evil in themselves, they will take away our ability to abide in His love if we do not learn to master them. One of the biggest things they hinder us from understanding and appropriating is how to *wait*.

In our fast-food society we are so accustomed to having things immediately that we believe that's the way it ought to be. Consequently, when we have to wait for God we become uncomfortable and indignant. We start doubting the truth of His love and promises. However, we need to realize that abiding in His love takes time and cannot be accomplished in three minutes, right after we've finished up with our "Three Minutes to a Better Body" DVD.

When we realize how vital it is to get in contact with God's love for us and see how many distractions have been set up around us to lure us away, it's perhaps tempting to feel discouraged. But we need to realize that the unprecedented busyness of our generation is actually creating a unique opportunity for us. You see, there is something powerful that happens when people say yes to Jesus in the midst of distractions. When you say yes to Jesus while surrounded by other options, it establishes a deep conviction inside of you which cannot be easily shaken. I did not ask my wife to marry me by saying, "SeaJay, here's the deal. There is no one out there who wants to marry me. You are the only one available—the only option I have. So, will you marry me?" Just the thought of it is pathetic. Marriage is a powerful union because it happens in the midst of options. "SeaJay, I have thousands of options, but *you* are the one I choose. You're the one I want to spend the rest of my life with. There is no one else out there who even closely compares to you." Now, I might have been a bit delusional thinking I had thousands of options, but you get the point.

Danny Silk, one of my spiritual fathers, taught me about the power of *yes*. He often points out that many people think the Christian life is a bunch of *nos*. Much of our discipleship has been based on teaching people how to say no. "No, I don't want that. No, I'm not going to go there. No, I'm not going to look at that." Then Danny explains that the Christian life was never meant to be a stream of nos. It is an overwhelming *yes* to Jesus that resounds in our spirits and drowns out all other options. Similarly, my marriage is not about my saying no to other options, but it's about my saying yes to my wife. After all, if the Christian life is to be lived with passion, it must be a life that has a positive goal.

TURNING YOUR AFFECTIONS

If Jesus is pursuing us and knocking on our door, then our responsibility is to open it when He knocks. Revelation 3:20 says, *"If anyone hears My voice and opens the door, I will come in to him and dine with him, and he with Me."* We must position ourselves in such a way that when He knocks, we open the door. His voice must be louder than all other voices in our lives. There can be no competition to the knock of Jesus. In fact, the more we encounter His love for us, the less anything else in our lives will have the strength to compare.

My favorite part of the day is when I get home from work. I walk in the door, put my bag down, and wait to hear, "Daddy's home!" I stand there with a smile on my face as the cutest kids in the world begin to emerge from different parts of the house. No matter what my children are doing, they drop it all and come running when they hear that I'm home. My boy might be playing with his super hero figurines, or my youngest daughter might be watching her favorite Barbie movie, or my oldest daughter might be playing her Nintendo DS. But it doesn't matter; they still come running. There is no competition in my home. I am confident that I can take on any super hero any day of the week. Barbie? Not a problem. I'll win every time over Barbie, Spiderman, or anyone else.

Jesus told us that we cannot enter the Kingdom unless we first become like children. When Dad comes home, nothing is more important than being with Him. When He knocks and when we hear His voice, we must come running. Everything else in our lives should pale in comparison to His knock. Sometimes His knock comes when we can make room to pull away and be with Him for extended periods of time. Other moments come when we are in class, or driving in our cars, or at the grocery store. No matter where it is, opening the door is simply a matter of focusing your attention toward Him. One night, right before I drifted off to sleep, the Holy Spirit showed up and said, "Banning, I am always available to you. All you have to do is turn your attention and affection to Me." Whether it's your daily devotional time or throughout your busy day, the issue is this: Will you turn your attention and affection to Him? As important as having a daily time with the Lord is, it's not the ultimate goal. The objective is to have the affections of your heart pointed in His direction no matter what is going on.

There are stories told of Smith Wigglesworth's prayer times with the Lord. I have heard that when he would pray, the weighty presence of the Lord would come so strong in the room that anyone else with him would leave for fear the glory might kill them. Wigglesworth understood how the affections of our heart would move Heaven. He said, "The moment you look up and are in a place of affection with Jesus the Heavens are opened." [5]

I find that the real value of my scheduled time with the Lord is that it helps to prepare me for my predominant goal, which is keeping my attention and affections on Him throughout the day. Andrew Murray says, "A man who seeks to pray earnestly only in the church or in the prayer closet spends the greater part of his time in a spirit entirely at variance with that in which he prayed. His worship was the work of a fixed place or hour, not of his whole being." [6]

Some of the sweetest times I've had with the Lord have not been scheduled spans of worship or prayer. In college I had a job as a valet, parking cars. Part of my time would be spent standing at the entrance to our valet parking lot to make sure no one parked there. All alone in the parking lot for hours, I would turn my heart to the Lord and just worship Him. I remember loving those intimate times of connection in the mall parking lot. If you are going to be a Burning One, one who lives a life of sustained passion for God, you have to learn to open the door when He knocks and turn your attention and affection toward Him.

When you stop for the Lord to find you, open the door to His knock, and turn your attention toward Him, you are giving Him the opportunity to love you, which He longs to do. This is what returning to your first love is all about. Years ago, there was a season in my life when the Lord emphasized this one thing repeatedly. It seemed as if every time I pulled away to be with Him, He only wanted to talk to me about how much He loved me. I would sit quietly with the Lord and ask, "God, what's on Your heart today?" And He would respond by saying, "*You* are on My heart today." Over and over again, He woke me up in the middle of the night to talk to me. I knew it was God waking me, so I would divert my attention to Him and ask Him what He wanted to share with me. Mostly I was expecting some incredibly deep revelation that I would be able to teach, but each time He gently said, "I just wanted to tell you I loved you."

"Okay. That's it? Anything else? Any deep revelation You want to share with me now that You woke me up?"

I loved His response: "Nope. I just wanted to let you know how much I love you." After a while, it was somewhat amusing to me when God woke me and we had this interaction. But I also began to understand what He was doing. He had to make sure I was completely saturated in the revelation of His love for me.

A big reason that I understood what God was doing with me was that I was a father. I want my children to know how crazy I am about them. I need them to know how much I love them *and* that I find so much pleasure in loving them. You have to catch this. I don't just enjoy having my children love me. I also find pleasure in loving my kids. Too many of us tell the Lord we love Him but never take the time to let Him love on us. Our prayer times consist of our pursuing God but never allowing Him to adore us. If, when I got home from work, my daughter came running up to me and said, "I love you, I love you, I love you," and then took off running to do something else, it would not be satisfying to me as a father. As much as I love to hear her say she loves me, it's not until I can sit down with her and express my love to her (usually through many sloppy kisses and smothering hugs) that I really feel satisfied. I love to love my kids! I want them to live a life secure in the fact that their dad is crazy in love with them.

I really enjoy working with young people, and I love to be around their passion. It inspires me. But sometimes I realize that in the midst of passionately pursuing God, they need to slow down and just let Him love on them. Most of our prayer times or worship occasions are about telling God how much we love Him, but we often don't take time to allow Him to express how much He loves us. As leaders, we are afraid that if we take time to do that we will begin to lose people to boredom. However, if we are to please Him, it is crucial that we avail ourselves so He can love on us. John and Carol Arnott and the Toronto Airport Christian Fellowship have done an amazing job teaching the Body of Christ how to receive the love of God. Their teaching on soaking prayer has radically changed the way people pray.

Nations and cities don't need Christians to be better organized. They don't need us to produce more impressive programs and run better ministries. What the cities and nations of the earth need are Christians who are burning with passion for Jesus. All of our organization and planning is irrelevant and powerless *unless* we are living lives of radical love for Jesus. We can only give away what we have. If we are called to represent Jesus to the world around us, we must have regular encounters with His love, because it's His love that He is trying to communicate through us to the world. His heart for people is the very reason He sent His only Son to die on a cross. The signs and wonders, the healings, and the prophetic ministry that are being released are all to point people to the revelation that God loves them. It's possible to miss that because unfortunately many of us have seen supernatural ministry without love. This is why Paul called us to the *"more excellent way"* of moving in power in First Corinthians 13—the way of love. In His Burning Ones, God is putting this more excellent way on display for the world to see.

JESUS CULTURE

CHAPTER 6

I JUST WANT TO BE A SON

Anyone who has ever taken a basic sociology course has more than likely heard of Charles Cooley. Considered the "Dean of Sociology," Cooley became famous for a concept he developed called the "looking-glass self," which means that your self-perception and self-esteem are largely determined by what you think the most important person in your life thinks about you. In particular, your self-perception and self-esteem are powerfully shaped when that most important person in your world actively expresses his or her opinion about you.

Tony Campolo, a sociology professor at Eastern College, tells a great story of a young boy. One day this young man came home from school with an "F" on his report card. He handed the report card to his mother. His mother, one of the most important people in his life, turned to him and said, "It just shows you they don't know how to educate a genius at that school!" I'm sure the boy walked away thinking, "That's right; I'm a genius. My mom believes I'm a genius, so it doesn't matter what that report card says. I am a genius."

As this new breed of revivalist begins to encounter the passionate love of Jesus and entwine their hearts intimately with Him—as He becomes the most important Person in their lives—their view of themselves begins to change dynamically. When the One who first conceptualized them and spoke them into being is given room to express His opinion about who they are, then His voice displaces the judgments and persuasions of other people, the enemy, and themselves. They begin to gaze into the looking glass of His heart and see themselves as He sees them. This has powerful results.

As you may be aware, our perception of ourselves manifests in the way we live life. If you believe there is greatness in you, your life will demonstrate that reality. Tragically, as I mentioned earlier in chapter two, many Christians have bought into the lie of insignificance. The enemy has assaulted them with the deception that their lives are insignificant and meaningless. One of the primary ways he achieves this is by portraying a picture in their minds where the circumstances in their lives, as well as in the world, are much too dire and overwhelming and they shrink in comparison. It is virtually impossible to watch the news without soaking up a barrage of devastating information that communicates the impossibility of change. Because of this, many people believe they cannot make a difference and their lives will never have an impact. *Why even try? The world is too big and messed up for my little life to change anything.* To be brutally honest, this message will paralyze them if they do not experience intimate encounters with God in which He enables them to realize the greatness inside them.

WHAT ARE YOU?

When I was 19 years old, I needed a car. My soon-to-be father-in-law called me up one day and offered to give me a 1985 Chevette he owned. I was completely ignorant about cars and thought any vehicle was better than none. However, when I went down to his house to pick up the Chevette I was in for quite a surprise. The Chevette was Chevrolet's attempt to copy the Ford Pinto. Imagine a football helmet with wheels and a steering wheel and less protection, and you're awfully close to the Chevette. SeaJay's dad took me to the parking lot where my new car was waiting for me. I rested my eyes upon a two-door hatchback with an oxidized sky blue paint job. Despite my initial reservations, I was still appreciative and gladly took possession.

On the three-hour trip back to Redding, I quickly learned about my new car. About an hour and a half into the drive I heard a sudden, loud bang. For a moment, I thought a huge rock had struck my car. But when I looked over my right shoulder to see if there was any damage, I discovered that it wasn't a rock. Rather, it was one of the back wing windows that had just blown off and landed on the side of the freeway. I drove on, stunned, not knowing what to do. I had never had a window tear out of a car before. "My window just flew off my car! Did that really happen?"

That was just the first of many quirks I had yet to discover. The ceiling fabric drooped in the car, so I had to strategically place push-pins to attach it back on. The hatchback never stayed open, so I made a custom broom handle to prop it up. The passenger door randomly flew open while driving and the stick shift dislodged and whoever was driving would have to find the proper spot and replace it so they could shift again. (I imagine that many of you reading this story are reminiscing fondly of a similar car you owned.)

Now, on the other end of the car spectrum is a Lamborghini. Recently I met a businessman in town who owns a Lamborghini Countach, one of three in the world like it and the only one in North America. This Lamborghini is worth a million dollars. A million dollars! To even think of a million-dollar car was crazy for me. The first question I asked him was, "Where do you park a million-dollar car? Do you just pull it into your garage next to the lawnmower and rakes?"

"No, no, no," he replied. "I have a special bubble I park it in." Apparently, there are bubbles you can buy in which to store your expensive car. You drive into the bubble and it seals to keep out all the condensation and moisture. I had never heard of a car bubble, probably because they cost more than my car.

I run into way too many Christians who have bought into the lie of insignificance and see themselves like my 1985 Chevette. In their perception, their lives don't seem very valuable, and they see so many things that don't work well. Because they believe they are small, frail, and worthless, they live lives of insignificance. But the truth is that we are not Chevettes. We are Lamborghinis. The way we determine the value of an item is to find out how much someone will pay for it. For example, if I wanted to find out how much my wedding ring was worth, I would go to different jewelry stores and ask them how much they would purchase it for. If one place offered me $500 and another proposed $1,000, then my ring would be worth $1,000 because someone was willing to pay that amount.

The cross should send us a glorious message about how highly God values us. He cherished you enough to pay the ultimate price— His Son's life. For much of the Church, Calvary is mainly about God forgiving our sins. We stop short of understanding and walking in the full purpose for His doing this, which was to restore us to relationship with Him and the identity that He intended for us from the beginning. If we are going to progress in our understanding of God's deep purposes for us, then it is vital to have ongoing encounters with our Father in which we hear Him declare over us and reveal who we really are.

OUR PURPOSE

There is a direct connection between our identity and our purpose. Scripture is filled with statements about the purposes that God has designed and destined for the lives of believers, and none of them are short of awesome. The fact that we were created to accomplish great things for God should convince us even more thoroughly that God sees us as Lamborghinis, not broken-down, pathetic Chevettes. God's first command to people was, *"Be fruitful and multiply; fill the earth and subdue it"* (Gen. 1:28). That command is still alive today. Jesus told us to *"...make disciples of all the nations..."* (Matt. 28:19). This is a big task that can only be accomplished through a people who believe their lives are worthwhile and they can contribute positively to the world around them. Much of the Church has been so overwhelmed with what is happening across the earth that they have concealed themselves in the hope of merely enduring the evil around them. But God didn't tell us just to survive; He commanded us to disciple nations.

Isaiah says:

> *Arise, shine; for your light has come! And the glory of the Lord is risen upon you. For behold, the darkness shall cover the earth, and deep darkness the people; but the Lord will arise over you, and His glory will be seen upon you* (Isaiah 60:1-2).

It is true that darkness is covering the earth. But that's not what God started with. He first told us to *"Arise, shine."* He didn't say, "Shrink away and hide your light in a corner." Deep darkness *is* covering the people, but God has an answer. His response to darkness covering the earth is a people who realize who they are in Jesus and arise in the earth with the glory of the Lord upon them. If you look throughout history, God has always had this answer for darkness. Notice that this answer is not just that His glory rises on His people, but that His people understand this revelation and stand boldly in the earth, allowing God to shine through them.

God wants to display His goodness, His greatness, and His glory through us. We are called to establish the reign of His Kingdom on the earth—to be light in darkness. But the plan of God can't be carried out without our cooperation, and we won't really be able to collaborate until we embrace the identity and purpose that He has spoken over us.

The lie of insignificance works directly against our ability to "Arise, shine." We are not on the earth to make it by the skin of our teeth and hold on until Jesus returns. We are here to establish His Kingdom.

NOT EMPLOYEES

One of the reasons the Church hasn't understood and responded to God's invitation to partner with Him by arising and shining in the darkness is that we still think He just wants good workers. If you've been in the Church for any length of time, I'm sure you've seen the tendency to think that our job is to work for God rather than to love God. But as I mentioned before, God is not our boss in Heaven just barking out orders for us to follow. He is a loving Father who longs to partner with His children. He sent His only Son to die on the cross— not to gather employees, but to establish a love relationship with people. He wants sons and daughters that grow to be mature lovers. Sons and daughters don't work for Him; they represent His nature to the world. It's going to be a partnership of love that sees the Church awaken to her call to partner with God.

John G. Lake, an apostle who ministered in the early 1900s and a man who was closely connected with the Lord, puts it this way:

> The wonder of redemption of Jesus Christ is revealed in the matchlessness of God's purpose to transform man into His very nature and image and fullness. Thereby men as sons of God become, bless God, the associates of the Almighty God, on His own plane of life and understanding.[1]

It takes most of us some time to comprehend just how God feels about us as His sons and daughters. I'm not sure if it's my personality or the fact I'm a male, but it wasn't the easiest thing for me to connect with the revelation that God is interested in loving me more than using me to change the world. I lean toward working for God in order to accomplish something together. I can wrap my brain around partnering with the Holy Spirit in order to take over the world. But when the Lord calls me just to sit and let Him love me, it's a little more of a challenge. As the Lord has done this with me, I have realized that He is an "ooey-gooey" God. He is not some cold and disinterested God.

Some people's view of God is much like Spock on Star Trek— calculating, emotionless, factual, and relationally disconnected. But this description couldn't be farther from the truth. Many people grew up with a father who never knew how to express his love for them. I met someone who only one time in her life heard her father say that he loved her. You can see why, in a society that has a hard time expressing true love, we perceive God like that as well. But He won't be satisfied with anything less than a relationship with you in which He can pour out His unfathomably endless love.

OUR CHOICE

Years ago when we first started doing Jesus Culture conferences, the Lord showed me something that changed my life forever. It was the morning session of one of our conferences, and I was scheduled to speak. I was sitting on the front row as nervous as could be. I was not at all confident about what I was going to preach. Judah Smith, one of the premier youth pastors in the nation from Seattle, Washington, had spoken the night before and just *tore it up*. It had been a phenomenal night—everything you would want at a conference. He shared an incredible word that was inspiring, practical, deep, and funny. Then he moved into a powerful time of ministry where he spoke out words of knowledge and prophesied over people. All over the room, people encountered God and were rocked by the prophetic words Judah spoke over them.

After such an incredible night, the next morning I sat there in the front row trying to enjoy worship but not able to because I was so anxious. I wasn't concerned because I desperately wanted God to minister His extravagant love to people. I was nervous because I didn't want to look stupid in front of Judah as I preached. As I sat there praying that my sermon would go well for all the wrong reasons, the Lord spoke to me. "Banning, you have a choice. You can either choose to be a preacher or a son. If you choose to be a preacher, you will be good sometimes and other times you won't be that good. But if you choose to be a son, you will always be good because you are a fantastic son."

That simple word from the Lord completely changed my attitude and my ministry. I knew I had to choose what I wanted to be.

I decided right then and there that I didn't want to be a preacher. I just want to be a son. And I'm a great son. I don't want to be a pastor, an itinerant minister, or anything else. I just want to be a son. Don't get me wrong; I want to be a great preacher and a great pastor, but I also realize that those things are not what motivate me. I'm pursuing being a great son, a son who knows that his Father loves him and in turn is in love with his Father. Everything else I do must be a result of that pursuit. I'm not called to work for God as a preacher; I'm called to be His son. I will preach as a son, but how I'm doing and who I am are not dependent on how well I preach—or not.

FOUNDED IN LOVE

God's work of establishing intimacy with His people as their first priority and thereby sealing us in our true identities is going to shift the ministry of His Church onto a different foundation—its true foundation. Everything that is not built upon that framework of intimacy and identity in God just doesn't have what it takes to last. The Lord told me early on in ministry that anything I do that is not founded in love is unstable. It is not bad to desire having an effective ministry that achieves great things for God as long as it's founded in your love for Him. I've been in ministry long enough to know that it can be very unpredictable. One year I can put on an event that is extremely successful and the next year hold the same event and have it fail miserably. But it's all okay as long as I keep my focus on what I really want to be, which is not a successful minister but a successful son. I want everything I do to be grounded in my love for my Father.

Even our ministry of love to other people—the second commandment—has to be founded in our love for God—the first commandment. I saw this as I was reading John 15 one day. *"If you keep my commandments, you will abide in My love…You are My friends if you do whatever I command you"* (John 15:10,14). Wow! I knew I wanted to be a friend of Jesus and abide in His love. But what was it that He was commanding me to do? Then I saw it, *"This is My commandment, that you love one another as I have loved you"* (John 15:12). In order for me to be a friend of Jesus and abide in His love, I have to do what He commands of me, which is to love others. Well, that's what I want to do. I want to love others. But what hit me was that, while I had always loved people, in connecting with this verse my love shifted to a new source. From that point, it was my desire to be a son and a friend of God that produced a love for others in me. My heart for people was to come from a place founded in my love for Him.

THE NEW EVANGELISM

What would it look like for an entire generation to live according to what Jesus thinks about them? What would it look like for a generation to be completely driven by a passionate love for God? As I write this, I can feel an excitement stirring within me as I imagine an entire generation who have made Jesus the most important Person in their lives, whose self-esteem is based on what He thinks about them, and who willingly rise up to shine with His glory in the midst of the darkness around them. This new breed emerging in the earth will live out this revelation.

I believe that because of what God is doing to reestablish the priority of intimacy in the Church, there is a confidence coming on the Body of Christ that has rarely been seen before. This boldness will be crucial if we are to carry out His purposes on the earth. For young people in particular, it will enable them to resist one of their greatest challenges—peer pressure. The battle over their identity is particularly strong in that stage of life. If they don't know what God thinks about them, they begin to look to others to tell them who they are. But a young person who knows who he or she is in God stands out in the crowd. Some of their peers will be drawn to these young revivalists, while others will be uncomfortable. God is enabling this generation to be true to who they really are so they are prepared to give an answer for the hope that is in them to the world around them.

This confidence, which is motivated entirely by their revelation of God's love, is going to bring about a major shift in the way the Church does evangelism. We are called to partner with God to see the knowledge of the glory of the Lord cover the earth and a billion souls swept into the Kingdom. I believe we are going to be able to fulfill this call because of the powerful revelation of God's love that is being released through this new breed of revivalist. It is the revelation of His love that will draw people to salvation.

Second Kings 7 tells a story that illustrates this new form of evangelism. The Syrians had besieged Samaria and had cut off all supplies of food. The city was experiencing a severe famine and in desperate need of deliverance. In the midst of this situation, there were four lepers hanging out by the gates of the city who came to a decision:

> *Now there were four leprous men at the entrance of the gate; and they said to one another, "Why are we sitting here until we die? If we say, 'We will enter the city,' the famine is in the city, and we shall die there. And if we sit here, we die also. Now therefore, come, let us surrender to the army of the Syrians. If they keep us alive, we shall live; and if they kill us, we shall only die"* (2 Kings 7:3-4).

So the lepers set off for the Syrian camp. Before they arrived, the Lord caused the Syrian army to hear the noises of chariots and horses, and the entire army fled in fear. In their flight they abandoned all their possessions. You can imagine the surprise of the four lepers as they strolled into a deserted camp full of food, wine, clothing, and gold. They did what anyone would do during a famine—they began to eat and drink as much as they could. But in the midst of feasting, they realized that what they were doing was not right:

> *Then they said to one another, "We are not doing right. This day is a day of good news, and we remain silent. If we wait until morning light, some punishment will come upon us. Now therefore, come, let us go and tell the king's household"* (2 Kings 7:9).

There's an entire generation who remain silent about the Gospel of Jesus Christ. Now, I've never believed that the strategy of making people feel guilty about not sharing their faith ever bears long-term fruit. I remember sitting in a youth service in which a group performed a skit that, in essence, simply put guilt on young people for not witnessing. I didn't like it then, and I don't like it now. I want to provide youth and young adults with an environment where they can encounter Jesus, feast on His extravagant love for them, and experience His limitless power. From that experience of abundant goodness, I believe a generation will arise whose evangelism will consist simply of inviting people into a feast they are already partaking from. People in famine always listen to those with food.

Every day, all around us, people are experiencing a famine of love and power. They have never sensed the true love that comes from God. They feel unable to change and stuck in life. They live surrounded by sickness, depression, pain, and hopelessness. It is as if a storm is raging inside them and they are powerless to calm it. They are searching for an answer and that answer resides in you.

One of my professors in college told us of an incident he had in a grocery parking lot. He was walking out to his car when he noticed a woman putting her groceries away in the trunk of her vehicle. On her car bumper was a sticker that read, "Jesus is the answer." My professor, being both intelligent and witty, stopped and asked her, "What is the question?"

The lady, slightly confused, turned to him and asked, "Excuse me?"

My professor asked, "If Jesus is the answer, then what is the question?"

Without hesitation she replied, "Mister, it doesn't matter what the question is. Jesus is still the answer!"

He is the answer! When you became saved, Jesus and His Kingdom took up residence inside you. Power over death, sickness, hopelessness, sin, depression, and addictions now lives in you. *You* possess the answer to every question inside of you. You have experienced a banquet that is worth sharing. As I previously stated, those in famine will always listen to those with food. The problem has been that we as the Body of Christ haven't looked like we have any food. We've looked no different to the world. Christians have been taught that the power of God is no longer available today, and they have protested against sinners rather than loving them. Thankfully, this is changing. If we appear just like the world, then why would they bother to come to us? They are ravenous for something they've never experienced— power and love. If they don't see power and love in us, then why would they listen to what we have to say? The world is drowning, and people are desperately seeking those who know how to swim.

LIFEGUARDS MUST BE SWIMMERS

I attended a great college, Vanguard University, in Southern California. Vanguard is located in Costa Mesa, California, just a few minutes from some of the most spectacular beaches in America. Newport Beach and Huntington Beach became regular destinations for my friends and me, and it was there that I learned how to surf. I wasn't very accomplished at surfing, but I was able to surf shoulder-high waves and have a blast. I went into full-time ministry after college, and a few years later we took the youth group to Southern California for a retreat. I hadn't been surfing since I was in college, so a few of my friends and I decided we'd get up early one morning and surf for an hour or two.

When we arrived at the beach the ocean looked a little crazy, but we decided to go out anyway. Big mistake! What we didn't know was that the largest swell to hit Huntington Beach in two decades was going to land that day. As you can probably guess, it didn't work out too well for me. I got caught in a set of waves in which I literally almost drowned. The current pulled me so strongly out to sea that I couldn't swim back in to shore, and I didn't have enough energy to get out past the waves that were coming in. So as wave after thunderous wave crashed in, I clung on for dear life and just tried to survive being repeatedly pushed under. The swells finally eased, and

I was slowly able to swim to shore. It was an experience I will certainly never forget and one I don't care to attempt again.

In order to become a lifeguard one must be an outstanding swimmer. It wouldn't make much sense if lifeguards did not know how to swim in the midst of waves. Can you imagine what might have happened if, while I was struggling to keep my head above water level, a well-intentioned guy came out to save me but then began to sink under himself? What if he didn't know how to swim that well and the waves scared him too? If I'm ever drowning I don't want someone in my position to come and save me; I want David Hasselhoff, the famous television lifeguard, to rescue me and tow me ashore.

Many of us in the Church are as disadvantaged as the people we are hoping to save because we don't know what God thinks about us or how He views us. Because we have not been secure in our identity, we have simply blended into the world. And even though the world around us is in the midst of drowning, they have not come to us because we look exactly like them. It is time for us to have such an encounter with God that our identity changes. Then we will stop worrying about what the world thinks about us and be able to welcome them into the feast we are experiencing.

SECTION IV

THOSE
WHO
PRAY

UNDERSTANDING THE SIGNIFICANT connection between a life of prayer and a life of power is paramount for the emerging revivalist. God awaits you and me in the secret place of prayer. There are distinctive realms available to us when we enter into His presence and intimately commune with Him. This is where He reveals His heart. And this is where the anointing to change nations is poured out and secured.

Fruitfulness in revival is preceded by a private prayer life. And full-blown revivals seem to always be prefaced by the faithfulness of persevering prayer warriors. Continuous fellowship with the Lord invariably centers our lives on His desires. It recalibrates our hearts to pursue His purposes.

Prayer will shift the atmosphere. And consistent prayer accesses realms of authority that nothing else can shake. All the resources and dominion of Heaven are available to us as we pray.

Several keys to sustaining prayer are shared in this section, such as intimacy, responsibility, belief, and revelation. Most importantly, we must understand that we don't need to strive to convince God, but prayer is simply an act of aligning our hearts with our Father—who is ready and willing to show up! He longs to respond. He finds our cries irresistible, because He finds you and me, His children, irresistible!

As revivalists, we have been given the divine mandate to stand amidst our generation and cry out for freedom and life. God desires to see His glory released. And all over the world, in every part of society, He is raising up prayer (or a praying people/Church) in the midst of darkness.

JESUS CULTURE

CHAPTER 7

THE SECRET PLACE

In the first chapter I told you about the fire for prayer that ignited in my heart when Lou Engle came to Bethel for the first time. My journey had begun a few years earlier, but that night I received an impartation from Lou that launched my prayer life to another level. In that meeting, I decided to be a man of prayer. I wanted, as David declared in one of his psalms, to *"give myself to prayer"* (see Ps. 109:4). I read about Frank Bartleman, the intercessor for the Azusa Street Revival, and how a "spirit of intercession had so possessed [him] that [he] prayed almost day and night."[1] He wrote in his book, *Another Wave of Revival,* how "My life was by this time literally swallowed up in prayer. I was praying day and night...Prayer literally consumed me."[2]

I desperately wanted to be "consumed" with prayer, but I knew I needed to learn how. I began to devour books on prayer and biographies of those who prayed—E.M. Bounds, Andrew Murray, Arthur Wallis, St. Teresa of Avila, Brother Lawrence, Frank Bartleman, Dr. Paul Yonggi Cho, and Leonard Ravenhill. I couldn't read enough about prayer. I was gripped by the stories of men and women who gave themselves to a life of prayer, and I wanted to follow in their footsteps.

Though I learned much from the testimonies of these saints, eventually I came to realize something. The best way to learn to pray is to pray. It's much like learning to be a parent. You can read countless books on the subject of parenting and glean wisdom from multiple experts, but the real learning begins the moment your beautiful child takes his or her first breath. That's when you enter your opening class in Parenting 101. Although I have read books on prayer, listened to sermons on prayer, and talked to people who pray, I learned to pray by actually setting time aside to pray and allowing the Lord Himself to teach me.

Jesus' disciples discovered this truth about prayer as well, as Andrew Murray explains in his book *With Christ in the School of Prayer*:

> The disciples had learned to understand something of the connection between Christ's wondrous life in public and His secret life of prayer. They had been with Him and had seen Him pray. They had learned to believe in Him as a Master in the art of prayer. None could pray like Him. And so they went to Him with the request, "Lord, teach us to pray."[3]

As I drew near to God during my own prayers in the months following Lou's visit to Bethel, I found myself making the same request of the Lord: *"Lord, teach [me] to pray"* (Luke 11:1). In response, He began to meet with me in prayer in a way I had not previously experienced. I started waking up early in the morning and slipping away to the Alabaster House—the prayer chapel at Bethel. I found that I felt *alive* in prayer. I also began to experience the reality Jesus spoke of when He said, *"But you, when you pray, go into your room, and when you have shut your door, pray to your Father who is in the secret place..."* (Matt. 6:6). God was waiting for me in the secret place of prayer. I entered a realm of God I never before imagined was available. At the time I didn't know it, but I was establishing what Mahesh Chavda describes as my "secret history with the Lord." God was meeting me in the secret place.

E.M. Bounds describes it this way: "The man—God's man—is made in the closet. His life and his most profound convictions are born in his secret communion with God."[4]

A history was developing between God and me that was not for anyone else. It was outside of the spotlight; no one really even knew it existed. What God and I were sharing in the secret place was not for any external ministry purpose. I just wanted more of Him and discovered that He also simply wanted to spend time with me. I spent hours in the secret place encountering His presence, worshiping Him, and hearing Him speak to me.

THE SECRET PLACE

God is waiting to encounter you in your secret place. He longs for a secret history with you. In my wife SeaJay's college years, she had a closet where the Lord would meet her. It was just a walk-in closet with clothes strewn all over the floor and shirts on hangers, but God was in that closet. SeaJay says that when she pulled away and walked into her closet, she became aware that God was waiting to meet her there. She would sit on her beanbag and wait to see what God wanted to do. Sometimes the Lord invited her simply to rest in the safety of His presence, and she would curl up and go to sleep. Other times He would take her into intercession through tears. And at times God took her away to a place He had made just for her. It was in the secret place that SeaJay learned to hear and trust her Father and know His ways. She was establishing a private history with God. SeaJay was experiencing what Andrew Murray calls us to: "To be alone in secret with the Father should be your highest joy"[5] because, "to the man who withdraws himself from all that is of the world and man and waits for God alone, the Father will reveal Himself."[6]

I remember having similar experiences when I went to the Alabaster House early in the morning. Many times I walked in to find that no one was around. As I opened the doors, tears would begin to stream down my face because I was walking into a room where I knew God was waiting for me. Your secret place may not be an exact location, but you enter it when you pull away from the world and find a place where you and God can establish a secret history together. It may involve spending hours in one location or only moments when you drop what you are doing and simply turn your heart to the One you've been longing for.

The new breed of revivalist emerging in the earth must be a generation that has established a secret life with Christ. The Lord is releasing an anointing to see entire cities and nations turn to God, but that anointing can only be secured in the secret place. In Second Kings 9, before Jehu was sent to end the reign of Jezebel he had to first get into the inner room to have oil poured on him. This represents the anointing of the Holy Spirit. Arthur Wallis points out that "there can be no substitute whatever for the anointing of the Holy Spirit; it is the one indispensable factor for the effective proclamation of God's message."[7]

There are some things you cannot get in public; you must press in for them in private. You can't go to conferences or have anointed men and women of God lay their hands on you to get this anointing. It is an anointing that results from encountering the Anointed One in the secret place, the inner room of prayer. Now, it's crucial that you go to conferences and have anointed people lay their hands on you. But you won't fully step into everything God has for you until you learn how to separate yourself to the Lord in prayer. Not one revivalist I have ever read about or met acquired his or her anointing through public gatherings. They received their anointing in the secret place of prayer. All of them have (or had) a secret life with God that, for the most part, they don't even talk about.

Lou Engle unintentionally gives us a peek into his secret life of prayer with God through a humorous story he tells. Lou is a general of prayer. He has an anointing to fill stadiums with praying believers and shift nations through intercession. For 20 years he gave his life to crying out for revival in the secret place with God. To this day, his heart burns to be in the secret place with God. His custom is to slip out of bed early in the morning and find a place to be alone with the Lord in prayer. Lou has seven incredible children, so you can imagine how challenging it is to find a secret place in his home! Often he jumps in his van and drives somewhere to pray.

One particular morning, he chose the parking lot of a local convenience store as his prayer closet. If you've seen Lou at all, you know he rocks back and forth while he prays. He says he's "priming the pump" as he rocks. On this occasion, he was having an amazing time in prayer and worship when he was startled by a knock on his window. Looking up, Lou saw a firefighter standing by the window and two large fire trucks parked behind his van. He turned his worship music down, rolled down his window, and curiously asked what was going on. The confused firefighter told him they had received an emergency call at their station about a man in a parked van who was having a seizure. Lou had to explain to the firefighter that he was not having a seizure; he was praying. It's one of my all-time favorite stories. Beyond being funny, it unveils the reality that Lou's life is fueled by prayer in the secret place with God.

HERITAGE OF PRAYER

Revivalists of the past established their lives in prayer and are shining examples of what God can do with one who prays. John Wesley spent two hours a day in prayer. E.M. Bounds writes of him, "One who knew him well wrote, 'He thought prayer to be more his business than anything else, and I have seen him come out of the closet with a serenity of face next to shining.'"[8]

Martin Luther, the father of the Reformation, said, "If I fail to spend two hours in prayer each morning, the devil gets the victory through the day. I have so much business I cannot get on without spending three hours daily in prayer."[9]

Evan Roberts, the young leader of the Welsh Revival, was a man of prayer. He would slip out of the revival meetings late at night "to pray all night in the quiet of his room."[10] S.B. Shaw recounts a three-month experience Roberts had:

I was awakened every night a little after one o'clock. This was most strange, for through the years I slept like a rock, and no disturbance in my room would awaken me. From that hour I was taken into divine fellowship for about four hours. What it was I cannot tell you, except that it was divine. About five o'clock I was again allowed to sleep on till about nine. At this time I was again taken up into the same experience as in the earlier hours of the morning until about twelve o'clock."[11]

Before this encounter Roberts was a man of prayer, but after this extended season of visitation with the Lord Roberts' prayer life was set ablaze at another level.

David Matthews, a participant in the revival, writes of Roberts, "Day and night, without ceasing, he prayed, wept, and sighed for a great spiritual awakening for his beloved Wales."[12]

Kathryn Kuhlman captured the secret of a life given to prayer more than anyone I've read about. This was not in the normal sense, for even some of her closest friends don't remember her having a regularly established time of prayer, but she had a heart that was always turned to the Lord in prayer. She said of her prayer life, "I've learned to commune with the Lord any time, any place. I take my prayer closet with me on the plane, in the car, or walking down the street. I pray always. My life is prayer."[13] Jamie Buckingham, her friend and biographer, writes of a time he saw her in a hallway behind stage before she ministered to the thousands who had come to receive a touch from God:

She was pacing, back and forth, head up, head down, arms flung into the air, hands clasped behind her back. Her face was covered in tears, and as she approached I could hear her. "Gentle Jesus, take not your Holy Spirit from me."[14]

As I mentioned earlier, the prayer life of Jesus was the model and inspiration for His disciples, as it was for every one of these notable revivalists. Jesus was a man of prayer and had a secret life with the Father. Luke states, *"But Jesus Himself would often slip away to the wilderness and pray"* (Luke 5:16 NASB). Mark also says:

> Now in the morning, having risen a long while before daylight, He went out and departed to a solitary place; and there He prayed (Mark 1:35).

My prayer is that there would be a generation of seekers who not only pursue Him corporately but also inquire of Him in the secret place of prayer. I'm encouraged when I see thousands of young people seeking the Lord together, but what I want to know is if that is happening in their bedrooms when no one else is around. Are they bringing to the corporate gatherings the momentum they have gained in the secret place? Have they captured the revelation that Charles Spurgeon talks about when he describes other work as "mere emptiness compared with our closets"?[15]

ALL ABOUT LOVE

I said earlier that the anointing that God is releasing for revival in this season will only be accessed and carried successfully by those who have established a secret history with the Lord. The primary reason for this is that revival is all about *love*. Signs and wonders, preaching, and any other aspect of supernatural ministry have one purpose only—to demonstrate the love of God to people and invite them into the love relationship He desires to have with them. Those who carry this power and demonstrate it to the world must be those who have that kind of kinship with the Lord. And this exchange is established in private. There are conversations my wife and I have that no one else will ever know about. Jamie Buckingham tells of how his backstage encounter with Kathryn Kuhlman praying ended: "I turned and fled, for I felt I had blundered into the most intimate of all conversations between lovers, and just my presence was an abomination."[16] This is the goal of our lives and the relationship our hearts yearn for with the Lord.

If you've established a secret harmony with the Lord, then when revival is happening all around you your foundation will be in place to steward it. Bill Johnson says, "Many times the busyness that revival brings becomes the enemy of revival."[17] It is easy to fall into a vortex of activity while working for revival, forgetting that revival is all about love. When this happens, our industriousness is disconnected from the thing that both motivates and gives it purpose. Without the supply of love behind our work, we will inevitably grow weary and probably give up. With love established in our lives, however, we will find our energy and passion renewed continually. One of my primary concerns in raising up a generation of revivalists is making sure they know how to pursue God privately as well as corporately.

A secret life with God always brings us back to our original purpose and passion. It recalibrates our heart. Whenever we find ourselves drifting away from the ultimate reason we are alive—to love God and be loved by God—the secret place realigns our priorities with love. It is what "keeps the main thing the main thing" in our lives. Your foundation of love must be deeper and wider than anything else in your life. Shasta Dam, one of Redding's claims to fame, is the second largest concrete gravity dam in America. Its hydraulic height is 522 feet. It holds back the massive amount of water in Lake Shasta, one of the largest man-made lakes in North America. But what is so impressive is not its height but its depth. It reaches 85 feet into the ground and is 543 feet thick at the base. Shasta Dam's base is actually wider than the dam is tall.[18] Similarly, if you are to step fully into your destiny, the depth of your understanding of the love of God must be incomparably larger than anything else in your life.

CONSTANT PRAYER

A few years ago I was flying back from a visit to the International House of Prayer in Kansas City, Missouri when the Lord spoke to me about establishing prayer in our youth ministry. I had gone to the IHOP at the invitation of Dwayne Roberts, the leader of One Thing Ministries, who had asked a handful of young leaders to meet and pray together for a few days. It was my first visit to IHOP. By that time, five years of 24/7 worship and prayer had been offered to the Lord from IHOP, and I was greatly impacted to see a ministry that had found keys for sustaining such a high level of intensity and devotion in prayer for so long.

I'm not sure why, but the Lord regularly speaks to me on planes. I think it might be because I'm closer to Heaven in a plane, but that's just a theory. Anyway, the Lord spoke to me about calling our entire youth ministry to give ourselves to prayer during the summer months. We called it "Summer of Prayer," we scheduled prayer meetings throughout the week, and we began to pray. The first meeting we had was on a Tuesday morning. Only a few people showed up, but we prayed, God came, and it was incredible.

About an hour into our prayer time, we began to pray for the school campuses in our city. I felt myself enter into a realm of authority over these campuses that was unfamiliar to me. It is sometimes difficult to explain feelings or experiences in prayer because it's in the spirit realm. But as I was praying I could sense a shift in the atmosphere of our prayers and they seemed to transition from the strength of a small hammer to a power-loaded demolition jackhammer! We knew the spiritual atmosphere was shifting over the campuses as we prayed and that principalities and powers were being displaced. I had touched that realm before, but I understood I didn't live there. Theologically I occupied that spiritual place but not always in practice. I believed I had been given authority over cities, but I had not pressed into or remained in that realm of authority through prayer. It became clear to me that there are realms of authority only accessed through consistent prayer. I had been praying for years, but I realized there was another level of prayer I had to press into if I was going to access the realm of dominion necessary to see entire cities saved.

What I experienced at that first prayer meeting continued through the summer as our youth ministry gave ourselves to prayer. During this season we were reminded of a dream that Lance Jacobs, Bethel's outreach pastor at the time, had received a few years earlier. In the dream, Lance was releasing people to minister in the city but was having no results. Nobody got saved, healed, or delivered. Then Linda McIntosh, one of our youth pastors and the resident lead intercessor, appeared next to Lance and said, "We must pray!" When she declared that, two fighter jets flew overhead. Lance then sent his team out into the city again, and this time the results were drastically different. People were getting saved, miracles were breaking out, and lives were being set free. We knew the Lord was calling us to a higher realm of authority that we had not tapped into yet—a realm that could only be accessed through prayer.

As I said, we found out right away that the cry of our hearts had to be *consistent* if we were to live in those new realms of authority. Jesus emphasized this repeatedly in His teachings on prayer. After instructing His disciples in the Lord's Prayer, He told them a story about someone asking a neighbor for bread at night. He said:

> *I say to you, though he will not rise and give to him because he is his friend, yet because of his* **persistence** *he will rise and give him as many as he needs. So I say to you, ask, and it will be given to you; seek, and you will find; knock, and it will be opened to you. For everyone who asks receives, and he who seeks finds, and to him who knocks it will be opened* (Luke 11:8-10).

The verbs in verse nine are all in present tense and could be translated, "Ask and continue to ask. Seek and continue to seek. Knock and keep on knocking." We are to persist in asking, seeking, and knocking. Jesus likewise taught through His parable about the persistent widow *"...that men always ought to pray and not lose heart"* (Luke 18:1). These stories and teachings of Christ took on greater relevance and significance for us as we experienced the power of consistent prayer.

The Book of Acts also provides us with a dramatic lesson on the importance of consistent prayer. Acts 12:2 records the death of James, the first apostle to be martyred, at the hands of King Herod. When he saw that James' death made the Jews happy, he detained Peter in prison with the intention of killing him as well. The church, mourning the loss of James, was not going to lose another one of their friends and leaders. Their response to the imprisonment of Peter was to pray: "...but constant prayer was offered to God for him by the church" (Acts 12:5). Notice that it was not just prayer but *constant prayer*. That night, Peter was miraculously set free by an angel and reunited with the friends who had been praying for him. Continuous prayer was the key for the believers in Acts to gain access to the realm of authority that was needed to see Peter set free.

It is important to remember that steadfast prayer isn't a matter of trying to convince God to answer us. If there was anyone who knew God's attitude toward us in prayer it was Christ, and He stated, *"And whatever things you ask in prayer, believing, you will receive"* (Matt. 21:22). What a staggering statement. Sit back and let that verse hit you. The Lord gave us a blank check signed by Him and promises that all the resources of Heaven are available to us if we pray. Andrew Murray writes, "The powers of the eternal world have been placed at prayer's disposal."[19] Yet Jesus clearly taught us that prayer must be sustained. If incessant prayer isn't required to get something to happen on God's end, we must conclude that it is required because of what it does on our end. Of course, much of what is going on when we pray is unseen and outside of our awareness. But the truth is that persevering in anything shapes us as well as the world around us.

Persistent prayer shapes our character, reinforces our tenacity, focuses our trust on the Lord, and increases our capacity to carry the authority and anointing that the Father has given us. At Bethel, we know that the increase in authority and anointing for healing that we have seen is directly related to sustained prayer.

FOUR KEYS: INTIMACY

How do you sustain prayer? If you have tried to abide in prayer for very long, you know that there is a reason Jesus mentioned the possibility of our losing heart. There are plenty of ways and plenty of reasons to become weary, frustrated, or disappointed and give up praying. You can only persist in prayer for so long on human zeal and effort alone. You might start praying because you feel guilty or a conviction that you have to, but it won't last long. A disciplined life, as important as that is, will only get you so far if you are going to give yourself to sustained prayer. During our "Summer of Prayer," we knew we needed to pray until we obtained what we were asking for, yet we knew we couldn't just "work harder" for it. Striving harder sounded like a recipe for burnout. So how were we to sustain prayer?

I believe four things are needed to sustain prayer. There are probably more, but these are the four things the Lord taught us to help us persevere in pursuing Him and praying for our city. The first is *intimacy*. The life of a believer is to be led by loving God and being loved by Him. Everything must flow from this. Andrew Murray, in sharing his secrets of prayer, stresses the importance of intimacy with the Father. "[Jesus] wants us to see that the secret of effective prayer is to have the heart filled with the Father-love of God."[20] Therefore, "The knowledge of God's Father-love is the first and simplest, but also the last and highest lesson in the school of prayer."[21] Anything that is not motivated by our love for God is unstable. Intimacy enables us to sustain prayer because it makes prayer a matter of spending time with the One you love, which is the natural expression and desire of love.

Prayer is hard to sustain if your view of God is anything but that of a loving Father. Many people view God as someone who is angry, sad, or disappointed with them. Who wants to hang out in prayer for a few hours with a God who is just going to let them know He isn't pleased with them? Nobody. Intimacy changes any misconceptions you might have about God because it brings you face to face with Him—a good Daddy. It's easy to sustain prayer with a God who is so extravagantly in love with you and is always telling you about it.

When our view of Father God comes into focus, we discover that His desire for His sons and daughters is not that we would be His servants but His friends and partners. A lot of believers still need to make this move from being employees in prayer to friends in prayer.

When I was 19 years old I worked for a short time on a painting crew. I was the grunt who had to do all the jobs nobody else wanted to do. It was brutal. I hated it. But here's the crazy thing. If one of my friends asks me to come over and paint his house with him, I do it with joy. I might be imitating the exact same job I did at 19, but it is completely different when I am working alongside my friend because I am not his employee; I am his friend, and we are accomplishing a task together. I don't *have* to; I *get* to.

We *get* to pray with our Friend Jesus. The Head Intercessor who lives to make intercession for us has invited us in to join with Him as He intercedes. Can you think of anything better than partnering with Jesus to see the dreams of His heart realized? Intimacy must be at the core of your prayer life, or it will either be short-lived or a nagging duty.

FOUR KEYS: RESPONSIBILITY

The second key to sustain prayer is *responsibility*. Many people don't sustain prayer for their city because they don't feel any responsibility for their region. If you live with a sense of responsibility you will live differently.

Let me give you an example. I have three gorgeous kids who are nine, six, and three years old. As a dad, I have the privilege of responding to late-night calls and cries. It might be a bad dream. It might be a request for water. It might be that they just decided to wake up at three in the morning. Whatever the reason is, when they call, I'm up and in their rooms seeing what I can do for them. They are my children and I have a responsibility to be aware of their needs and listen for their cries.

However, if I were to stay the night at one of my friend's houses, things would be different. If I woke up to the cries of my friend's children in the middle of the night, I would more than likely find ear-plugs, roll over, and go back to sleep. Why? Because those children aren't my responsibility. I know my friend will do his "Daddy role" and get up to check out what is going on. I respond differently to their needs than to my own children's needs.

It is the same with your city. If you don't take responsibility for your city or campus or workplace and the people in it, then when something happens you will roll over and fall back asleep instead of going to prayer. You won't disengage because your heart is evil but because those aren't your kids. You haven't taken responsibility for your city. People sustain prayer for things they feel responsible for. Many people have a hard time upholding prayer because they have no real sense of responsibility for their city or their nation.

Second Kings 4 tells of an interaction Elisha had with a widow. The creditor was coming to take her two sons to be his slaves because of the debt left behind by her husband, so the widow cried out to Elisha to intervene. Partnering with the widow, Elisha supernaturally provided the resources needed to pay off the creditor and save her sons. What I want you to catch is that the widow's cry was birthed out of a sense of responsibility for her sons. She lifted up her voice because her sons were headed into slavery. We also must lift up our voice in a cry to Heaven for those around us whose lives are being taken captive.

If you have ever been to TheCall, you have encountered a company of people who have taken responsibility for their nation.[22] At TheCall, people stand for 12 hours before the Lord, fasting and praying, often with the sun beating down on them or the rain falling. They aren't there just to be intimate with the Lord; they are there to cry out for their nation, of which they have taken ownership. It's not okay to sit back while unjust laws are passed, violence increases, babies are aborted, people live in poverty, and racism still exists in our nations. These issues must drive us to prayer as we take respon-sibility for our nations and call out for a great outpouring of the Holy Spirit to see them turn back to God.

FOUR KEYS: BELIEF

The third key to sustained prayer is a "theology of breakthrough." Mike Bickle coined this phrase when describing one of their keys to sustaining prayer at the International House of Prayer. Put simply, you've got to believe God is going to show up when you pray. Again, Andrew Murray advises in the ways of prayer: "We may and must confidently expect an answer to our prayer."[23]

Many people, without realizing it, go through the motions of prayer with no power because they don't really believe their prayers move the heart of God. But the truth is that we have a God who is even more eager to show up in our city than we are for Him to show up. Isaiah says that God *"...acts for those who wait for Him"* (Isa. 64:4). That means God is moved to action on behalf of those who seek Him in prayer.

Sustaining prayer isn't so arduous when you believe God responds to your prayer. You trust breakthrough will come because God answers prayer. Our faith is not in our ability to pray but in His ability to answer. It may take a while. It may seem like God is slow. But He will answer because you are praying. Your ability to continue praying when it seems that God is not listening is in direct relation to your knowledge of His character. George Mueller, when asked if he had any unanswered prayers, confidently replied, "No. That is except for one. But it will be. How can it be any other way? I am still praying."[24] The unanswered prayer was for the conversion of a friend's son. At Mueller's funeral that son gave his life to Jesus. Mueller was a man confident in the character of God and confident in the effect his prayers had to move Heaven.

FOUR KEYS: REVELATION

The fourth key to sustained prayer is *prophetic revelation.* This has been a huge influence in our ministry. When the Lord speaks to us through dreams, prophetic words, Scriptures, and other prophetic experiences, He's providing fuel for our fires of prayer. These things give direction and let us know we are on the right track. Any time we begin to feel weary in our prayers, the Lord is faithful and sends us a dream or a prophetic word or enlivens a Scripture for us, and faith to keep pressing in ignites again in our hearts. It is one of the most exciting, dynamic aspects of our interactions with the Lord. It makes prayer an adventure.

Beyond learning to *receive* prophetic revelation, we've had to learn how to *carry* prophetic revelation. It is one thing to hear a prophetic word; it is a whole other thing to carry that prophetic word in prayer. TheCall, the International House of Prayer, and Bethel Church all have great value for the prophetic and have made it their practice to bring prophetic words back to the Lord in prayer consistently. I have pages and pages of prophetic words that have become fuel for my prayer life. I have words that I received in my teenage years. I am always going back to them, reviewing them, and praying through them as I remind myself and the Lord of what He said. I heard a preacher say once, "Prayer is really just us finding out what God wants to do and then going back to Him and asking Him to do that." Through prophetic revelation, the Lord draws our focus to what He is doing so we can hit the mark in prayer. Our faith to pray is greatly augmented when we know we are in agreement with the Lord on a particular issue.

We have been pursuing a generation to be saved and transformed in our city for years. It is a passion of ours that we have embraced in prayer with all of our heart. Years ago the Lord spoke to us about our responsibility to pray for the salvation of 15,000 young people in our region. Shortly after God said this, I was walking through our church lobby when I glanced up and saw a magazine cover that took me by surprise. On the front cover was the headline in bold letters: "15,000 Students to Change the World." I had the cover framed and hung in our office because I knew the Lord was confirming to us our mandate to pray for and actively pursue the salvation of 15,000 young people.

We had been carrying that word for years when Rachel Jacobs shared a dream with me. In the dream, a lady was prophesying to Rachel. She said, "Adam and the 15,000 are coming. Adam and the

15,000 are coming." In the dream, Rachel knew what this lady was saying was important and was going to happen. When she awoke, she was confused and couldn't make sense of the dream because she didn't know anyone named Adam and she could not figure out the significance of the number 15,000.

When she shared the dream with me I instantly knew what it meant. The Lord was encouraging us through a prophetic dream to continue to press in for the salvation of 15,000 young people. I also knew Adam was representative of Jesus and how a generation will bear His image. In First Corinthians, while talking about the Last Adam, who is Jesus, Paul says, "...*we shall also bear the image of the heavenly Man*" (1 Cor. 15:49). That dream became even more fuel for the prayer movement among our youth.

God is intent on saving the lost in our cities. As we will discover in the next chapter, those who pray must receive a revelation of how irresistible their prayers are to a God who calls Himself *Father*.

JESUS CULTURE

CHAPTER 8

COME ON DOWN!

I hate to admit it, but I was once addicted to the television show *The Price Is Right*. It was the summer before my sophomore year of high school. I hadn't yet gone for my driver's license, so I was generally stuck at home and found myself waking every day at 10:00 A.M. to turn on the television to the words, "Come on down! You're the next contestant on *The Price Is Right*." Little did I know that my hours spent watching that show over the summer would pay off years later. Let me explain.

My friend and former college pastor, Daniel Miller, had a vision in which God was in the audience on *The Price Is Right*. He saw the Lord sitting on the edge of His seat, waiting excitedly for the announcer to call the name of the next contestant. When he shared this vision with me, the Lord began to speak to me. Because of my vast knowledge of the show, I couldn't get over the profound revelation of God this vision gave me.

If you've ever seen *The Price is Right*, you know how it works. On this game show, contestants guess the price of certain items, and whoever estimates the closest figure without exceeding the actual price proceeds to the next round. Before the game begins, Rod

Roddy, the show's announcer, pulls a random name from the studio audience to compete in the game. Right before he broadcasts the name, the entire studio audience is expectantly waiting on the edge of their seats. Each one of them is hoping: "Come on, pick me! This is it! I know I'm going to get called!" Many of the audience members are wearing shirts that say something like "I love Bob Barker" (the show's host) or "It's My Birthday Today."

Then Rod Roddy, in dramatic fashion, announces the next contestant: "Jill Johnson, come on down! You're the next contestant on *The Price is Right!*" The camera then begins frantically scanning the audience for Jill Johnson. You can always tell who the next contestant is because she is the one standing up, hands flailing in the air, screaming at the top of her lungs and looking completely foolish. Then Jill begins to make her way forward, still shrieking, gives some high fives to random audience members, and runs down the aisle to the front. In my entire summer of watching the show, I cannot remember one time it didn't happen like that. Not one person, when his or her name was called, casually stood and began to stroll nonchalantly down the aisle to the front like it was no big deal. They always rushed to the set with great enthusiasm.

That was the vision Daniel Miller had—God on *The Price is Right*. Can you see it? There's God, on the edge of His seat, excited and eager to be called on. Psalm 145:18 says, "The Lord is near to all who call upon Him, to all who call upon Him in truth." Unfortunately, a lot of people in the Church have suspected that the exact opposite is true of God. I've been in prayer meetings where I wasn't sure we really believed God wanted to show up. For some reason, we acted like our job was to convince God to do something He really didn't want to do. Apparently, our prayers were supposed to twist His arm to coerce Him to respond and send revival. We cried out to God but were never certain if He would reply or not.

I believe that the root of this perception of God is a doubt that He is truly *good*. My prayer is that God would release a greater revelation of His goodness toward us. We serve a great God who longs to give us the Kingdom; in fact, He finds pleasure in giving us the Kingdom (see Luke 12:32). Every good and perfect gift comes from Him (see James 1:17). He's the Giver of good gifts. He is a good God and does good things. As I said in the last chapter, God wants to show up in response to our prayers even more than we want Him to.

But here's the thing: The revelation of God's goodness is something that really only opens up to us in relationship with Him. If I give a homeless person a few dollars he could say I did something good, but he couldn't necessarily know that I was a good person. He would have to get to know me to know if goodness was part of my character. And to get to know me at the level of my heart and character he would have to become my close friend. Close friends are the ones I trust with my heart. The same is true of God. The entire world experiences the goodness of God every minute of every day. All that we are and have are gifts from Him. But our awareness of His goodness is in direct relation to how well we know Him. The closer we draw to His heart, the more we realize how good and extravagant He is toward us.

THE REVELATION OF FRIENDSHIP

In Christ, God calls us friends with whom He shares His secrets (see John 15:15; Luke 8:10). The new breed arising in the earth has stepped into this reality. The revelation of His goodness through friendship with Him has freed them from feeling the need to manipulate God through their prayers. Instead, they believe God is eager to show up when they call on Him. They know they are not trying to convince God but to partner with Him to see His desires fulfilled in the earth.

When we have a distorted view of God our prayers will inevitably be misdirected and ineffective. I submit that we have not seen the true power of prayer in much of the Church because too many of us think that God is an angry God who wants to punish people rather than visit them with His kindness, mercy, and grace. Some don't go as far as to say God is outright angry, but they think He is extremely frustrated and disappointed with the world and with us.

This distorted perception of His attitude toward us leads us to believe our responsibility is to work as hard as we can so He doesn't reveal how disappointed He really is.

I believe that much of the repentance that happens in prayer meetings is rooted in this perception of God. I've been in prayer meetings where all we've done is repent. Entire prayer meetings have consisted of telling God how sorry we were for being sinners and profusely apologizing that all the people in our city were sinners. Eventually I began to realize that one of the main reasons we were repenting was that we didn't actually think God wanted to show up. We had a concept of a God in Heaven who was so disgusted with our sinful condition that the last thing He wanted to do was show up in the middle of such an unrighteous group. In fact, He wasn't going to come because He needed to prove the point that He was not happy with us. But maybe if we could just let God know we were really, really, really sorry, He would feel bad enough for us and show up even though He didn't want to.

Please hear me; I believe in repentance. And we had better not take advantage of the extravagant love and grace of God. We must deal with sin in our lives and get rid of things that grieve His heart. Sin absolutely hinders and affects our connection to God. We can't live just any life we want to and expect God to reveal Himself when we pray. However, I don't believe in repentance when it's motivated by a wrong concept of God. We must repent with the conviction that the Father longs to respond to our cries even though we aren't perfect. Biblical repentance flows from the understanding that God sincerely wants to respond to our prayers and that He insists on confronting those issues in our lives that hinder His presence. In other words, God is actually the initiator of biblical repentance, and He invites it with His *goodness*: "...*the goodness of God leads you to repentance*" (Rom. 2:4).

God is eager to answer when we call. He loves to respond to our genuine and honest prayers, and He longs for His Church to catch the vision of His eagerness and willingness to come. Again, I can see Him in Heaven on the edge of His seat eagerly waiting for us to declare, "God, come on down!" He's sporting His shirt that says, "I Love My Church," and when the Church calls Him, He leaps out of His seat cheering for joy. He looks at the angels gathered around His throne and says, "They called Me, and I'm going down!" Perhaps He even high-fives some of the angels on His way down.

This is why my friend Daniel's vision so gripped me. We are praying to a God who is ready and willing to show up. We don't have to convince Him. We just have to call and He'll come. I believe that the current prayer movement is being propelled by this revelation. Why else would we give ourselves to prayer day and night? We can only do it if we know He longs to respond to our prayers.

This new breed of revivalist is beginning to connect with His heart, which is burning with passion for cities like San Francisco, Las Vegas, Amsterdam, London, Brisbane, Seoul, New York, Moscow, Jerusalem, Baghdad, and other cities in the earth. God is sending this new breed of revivalist into families, businesses, campuses, neighborhoods, and cities all over the world, armed with the revelation of His goodness and the confidence that He will show up when they pray.

Some of my close friends are giving themselves to prayer in Southern California. Jake and Nicci Hamilton and Eddie and April Brown lead prayer houses that are contending for revival and praying for a shift in the nation. Jake leads a dynamic prayer ministry called the Refuge House of Prayer. For six hours a day they gather, praying for revival. They pray because they believe God's heart is burning for their city, state, and nation. Eddie Brown leads an influential prayer ministry in San Diego called the Justice House of Prayer. They have been praying faithfully five days a week at the University of California at San Diego. They stand on the head of a sidewalk that is laid in the shape of a snake winding up a hillside. It represents false ideology in the nation and they are praying to see the delusions replaced with the truth of God. They pray because they believe God answers them. Both of these radical couples and the companies they lead have given themselves to a life of prayer, confident in the One who answers.

THE REVELATION OF SONSHIP

The reason God is so excited to come when we call is that He has adopted us as His sons and daughters. The revelation of who God is to us as our Father will infuse our prayers with faith like nothing else. We find this revelation in what Jesus modeled for us. One of the most stunning teachings of Jesus is that we can relate to God as a Father in the same way Jesus related to Him as a Father. When Jesus instructed His disciples how to pray, He told them to say, *"Our Father in Heaven"* (Matt. 6:9). In doing so, He was connecting the disciples to God the Father in the same way that He was connected to God the Father.

Can you imagine Jesus doubting whether the Father would show up when He prayed? Jesus knew that if He simply asked, His Father would send legions of angels to interrupt His whole plan of sending His Son to the cross (see Matt. 26:53). There was no question whether the Father would answer Him. We are to have the same attitude and for the exact same reason—we are sons and daughters of God. The implications of this truth are staggering and will radically affect the way you pray. Andrew Murray puts it this way, "Live as a child of God and you will be able to pray and most assuredly be heard as a child."[1]

When Jesus taught on the Father heart of God, He said:

> Or what man is there among you who, if his son asks for bread, will give him a stone? Or if he asks for a fish, will he give him a serpent? If you then, being evil, know how to give good gifts to your children, how much more will your Father who is in Heaven give good things to those who ask Him (Matthew 7:9-11).

In this statement, Christ defined prayer as an interaction between a child and a father. He acknowledged that there is a difference between the way human fathers treat their children and the way God treats us. But the difference is that the absolute best that human fathers give their children pales in comparison to the good things God gives to us. You must have this revelation of your heavenly Father's attitude toward you. The truth is that God finds your cries *irresistible* because He finds you, His child, irresistible.

I have three small kids, and as a father I understand the power of my children's cries. When Ellianna, my first child, was a little over a year old, without fail she would wake us up every night around 2:00 A.M. We had fallen into the habit of allowing her to come and sleep in our bed with us. After a few months of having a tiny foot in my back all night, we decided to transfer her back to her crib to sleep. SeaJay and I were rookie parents, so we asked around to find out the best way to go about this transition. Almost everyone we spoke to explained that we needed to let her "cry it out" when she woke up in the middle of the night. They warned us that she might cry for extended periods the first few nights, but eventually she would learn to go back to sleep on her own and stay peacefully in her room all night.

We set aside three days that we knew we could devote to this process and began to prepare ourselves for the nights of extended crying. We were serious about encouraging her to sleep through the night. The first night rolled around and, sure enough, right at 2:00 A.M. she began to cry. I walked into her room, told her I loved her, and said that now she was a big girl who had to stay all night in her own bed. Then I calmly exited the room, leaving our screaming child to exhibit her wide range of vocals. I walked into our room, plopped on the bed next to my wife, and turned on the lights. I could tell my wife was already having a hard time, so I encouraged her to resist the desire to go and rescue our baby girl. I was certain she was the weaker one of us, and I knew she needed my strength. I declared that we had to persevere and not give in, so we settled in for the battle.

Then, out of nowhere, we were blindsided by something. I, in particular, was totally unprepared for it. About ten minutes into this ordeal, my little girl began to do something she had never done before. In the midst of her loud sobs, she began to yell, "Da Da...Da Da...Da Da!" I slowly began to melt in my bed, just dying inside.

My little girl needed me! How could I leave her in bed when she obviously needed her daddy? Finally, I was conquered. I turned to my wife and said something to this effect: "I cannot believe you are making her sleep in her room. I am going to get her. She needs me!" I walked into her room, picked her up, and told her she could sleep with us forever.

I believe that when my daughter called my name, I experienced in a small measure what God feels when we call on Him. Paul tells us, *"For you did not receive the spirit of bondage again to fear, but you received the Spirit of adoption by whom we cry out, 'Abba, Father'"* (Rom. 8:15). When we call out to Father God, we are actually demonstrating that we belong to Him and that His Spirit has taken up residence in us. We are demonstrating that we have put our faith in Him. Somehow the word "faith" has come to mean agreeing with a set of statements about God. But faith is a relational word. It is trust in a Person—the most trustworthy Person in existence. When we lean on Father God, He has to come through for us. This is why faith moves God like nothing else. Faith cannot be denied and always achieves results.

Having our prayers answered is entirely a matter of knowing and trusting our Father. There is a level of confidence you will pray with when you know the goodness of the Father's heart; you have a boldness that knows His heart, that understands His will, and that He is faithful to answer. Consider the statement by the apostle John:

> Now this is the confidence that we have in Him, that if we ask anything according to His will, He hears us. And if we know that He hears us, whatever we ask, we know that we have the petitions that we have asked of Him (1 John 5:14-15).

His will is to come when we call on Him. When we approach Him as children, He turns to us as a Father. Dann Farrelly, one of the pastors at Bethel, once gave a message on the Prodigal Son that he entitled "The Running Father." What a great description of our God. He is a Father who, when He sees us turn our hearts to Him and call on Him, begins to run toward us with great passion and love. God the Father finds the cries of His children irresistible. It's how He designed it all. This is why the cry of a surrendered child of God is so powerful—it moves all of Heaven because it touches the heart of the Father. He's on the edge of His seat just waiting for His children to lift up their voices and call on their Daddy.

CARRIERS OF INCENSE

The revivalists God is raising up and sending into the world will live in the revelation of the Father heart of God and will walk with childlike faith. Because their cries move Heaven, God is sending them into the world as *carriers* of prayer—those He can strategically send to cry out to Him in the places that need Him to come the most.

In Numbers 16, we read about a plague that was released among the people of Israel because of their rebellion. In response, Moses and Aaron ran to the tabernacle, where Moses instructed Aaron: *"Take a censer and put fire in it from the altar and put incense on it"* (Num. 16:46). Aaron did as Moses instructed, and then he headed out into the midst of the plague to stand between the *"dead and the living"* (see Num. 16:48). When he came into the plague carrying the fire and incense, the plague ceased.

Notice that Moses and Aaron didn't stay in the tabernacle and intercede for the people. Moses sent Aaron *into the midst of the plague* with fire and incense. There has been a plague of darkness released on a generation, and God's answer is to send His children running into the heart of that plague to stand between the dead and the living. As revivalists, we have been given the mandate to stop this plague. You are a plague terminator. But we will not go into the plague unequipped. God is sending us with passionate love and prayer (fire and incense). All over the nation, in every part of society, God is raising up prayer in the midst of the plague. On campuses, in businesses, in neighborhoods, in every realm of society, God is establishing those who carry incense. It is His plan to see the plague stopped and His glory released.

The Lord gave us a vision for our ministry Campus Awakening a few years ago. Part of that vision was releasing a generation of youth and young adults onto their campuses to lift up their voices in the midst of the plague and cry out to God for revival. On one junior high campus, our Campus Awakening group consisted of one seventh grade girl named Ruby. Along with the teacher who was sponsoring the Campus Awakening and a small local church, Ruby planned a talent show to reach out to her campus. They signed up a few students to participate in the show, arranged for a youth pastor from Fresno to share his testimony of God saving him out of gangs as a teenager, and set the date.

They expected around 20 kids to show up and bought enough pizza and soda to feed them. But the day of the event, students and teachers just kept flocking into the cafeteria. Over 200 students and 15 school staff showed up to see the show. At one point, the MC directing the show took a moment to acknowledge the Campus Awakening group for putting on the event. He said, "Everyone in the Campus Awakening club stand up." Ruby stood up. The MC looked around and said, "Come on, don't be shy. Stand up." Ruby said, "No, it's just me."

After the guest speaker shared the Gospel, between 70 and 80 kids responded to his invitation to give their hearts to the Lord. Teachers were saying that it was the best school assembly they had ever seen. And it happened because God sent one fire-filled seventh grade girl to her campus with incense. When she cried out to God in the midst of the plague of darkness, He couldn't stay away. If God will show up at the cries of a seventh grader, what will He do when you call out to Him in dark places?

SECTION V

HEALING REVIVALISTS

JESUS CULTURE FOLKS know and walk in the revelation that they are indeed the light of the world! They understand their personal responsibility to unveil the reality of the Kingdom in and through every aspect of their lives. They are taking the ministry of their Lord out into the world! They are going public!

Understanding that light is always superior to darkness, they are emboldened to display God's power wherever they go. They deny the strategies of the enemy to restrain and diminish their enthusiasm, their faith, and their courage. Their close friendship with the Lord and confidence in His Word are their encouragement, as they ignore the allure of the world's opinions, and shine forth their light. Pushing aside the fear of failure, they continue to press on and embrace each situation as an opportunity to grow.

You and I are invited to manifest the Kingdom—in power! When people ask who we are, we should be able to direct them to what we *do* as evidence of the One we represent! Enabled by the Holy Spirit, we can introduce Jesus upon a platform of demonstration. This extreme boldness to transform the world only comes as we abide in Him and stretch out our steps into the unknown. As history makers we must take risks, and our radical obedience is the key to supernatural fruit!

JESUS CULTURE

CHAPTER 9

TIME TO GO PUBLIC

One of the most popular testimonies to come out of Bethel in the last ten years was from one of my dear friends, Chad Dedmon. Chad was on his way home late one evening when he decided to swing by a local grocery store in Redding to pick up a snack of donuts. On his way to the donut aisle, he noticed a lady in the checkout line who was wearing hearing aids. So he did what is becoming normal for this new breed of revivalist: He stopped and asked the woman if he could pray for her hearing to be healed. She explained that she had significant hearing loss in both ears and graciously accepted Chad's offer.

Chad prayed a simple but powerful prayer and then asked the lady if she didn't mind taking out her hearing aids to test her hearing. (This act of faith—having someone test out their healing—is a critical thing to do if you are going to see people healed.) The lady removed her hearing aids. Chad stepped to one side of her, where she could not see him, and quietly asked, "Can you hear me?"

She said, "Yes, I can hear you."

Chad moved back further. "My name is Chad."

She responded, "Your name is Chad."

He stepped back even farther. "My favorite food is pizza."

She returned, "Your favorite food is pizza." By now, tears were streaming down her face as she realized she was hearing clearly without the assistance of her hearing aids. She had been healed.

The cashier, who had watched all this unfold before her, began to cry too as she realized what had just happened in her checkout line. Chad turned to the cashier and said, "God is here right now healing people. Is it all right if I get on the intercom system and tell people what God is doing?"

With tears still in her eyes the cashier replied, "Of course."

Chad grabbed the microphone and boldly announced, "Attention, shoppers. God just healed this lady of deafness." Then he had the lady get on the microphone and share her testimony of being healed. Seizing the moment, Chad began to give words of knowledge over the intercom system. "If you have carpal tunnel syndrome or if you are experiencing hip problems, God is here right now and wants to heal you. Come to cash register ten if you want to be healed."

At this point people were peering around the aisles to see what was going on. A small group began to form at cash register ten. As the crowd came together, a lady scooted up on a motorized shopping cart. She looked at Chad and said, "You mentioned someone with a hip problem. Well, that's me. My hip is in severe pain, and I am scheduled to go in for hip surgery." Chad asked if he could pray for her and release the power of God to her. After a short prayer, Chad asked if she would stand up and test out her hip. She quickly responded, "No way. When I walk on my hip, it causes excruciating pain." Chad explained that it was important to put an action to her faith and test out her healing. She reluctantly got up, and as she began to walk she started screaming. She turned to Chad with a huge smile on her face and declared, "There is no pain! There is no pain!"

Then, from the back of the crowd, a man pushed his way forward with his wrists held out in front of him. He reached Chad and said, "I'm the one with carpal tunnel syndrome. I have had it for two years. I've been in so much pain that I am unable to play the piano, which is what I do for a living. I teach piano lessons and am a concert pianist."

Chad reached over, laid his hands on the man's wrists, and prayed for him to be healed. The man began to shake his hands up and down as he belted out, "My hands are on fire! My hands are on fire!" Instantly, the Lord healed him. His pain left and full mobility was restored in his wrists.

Chad spoke to the crowd that had just witnessed these two people receive a healing touch from the Lord and told them about Jesus the Healer, who was revealing His presence and power right there and then. After giving a brief talk about the King and His Kingdom, Chad asked if anyone would like to give their lives to Jesus; if so, he told them to raise their hands. Throughout the crowd, hands began to raise as people surrendered their lives to Jesus.

LIGHT YOUR WORLD

As I shared earlier in the book, I am thoroughly convinced that God's heart is longing for entire cities to turn to Him and be saved. This has been our heart in Redding for years. We have been pressing in to see our city and region saturated in the glory of God and praying that everyone would experience His goodness and love. Because of this, the Lord has been releasing simple but profound strategies to us for reaching our city and region. One of these strategies comes from both Matthew and John.

> *Now as Jesus passed by, He saw a man who was blind from birth. And His disciples asked Him, saying, "Rabbi, who sinned, this man or his parents, that he was born blind?" Jesus answered, "Neither this man nor his parents sinned, but that the works of God should be revealed in him. I must work the works of Him who sent Me while it is day; the night is coming when no one can work. As long as I am in the world, **I am the light of the world**"* (John 9:1-5).

> ***You are the light of the world.*** *A city that is set on a hill cannot be hidden. Nor do they light a lamp and put it*

under a basket, but on a lampstand, and it gives light to all who are in the house. Let your light so shine before men, that they may see your good works and glorify your Father in Heaven (Matthew 5:14-16).

As you can see, Jesus makes two very similar statements in these passages. In John 9 He said, *"I am the light of the world,"* and then in Matthew 5 He said, *"You are the light of the world."* This difference is small but massive in meaning. We mustn't emphasize what Jesus said about Himself at the expense of missing out on what He spoke over us. Jesus turned to us and said *"you."* That word "you" creates personal responsibility. I previously explained the importance of personal responsibility in sustaining prayer, and it is just as important here. Too many people have not taken responsibility to be the light of the world.

Light reveals things. The light carried by every believer is the revelation of our King and His Kingdom. Being the light of the world means that we are all responsible to unveil the reality of that Kingdom through every aspect of our lives. It is our duty and privilege. This is the Church's ministry in the world. For too long pastors have taught that real ministry happens through the "anointed" men and women of God in vocational ministry. We have not empowered believers to be full-time ministers no matter what they are doing.

This is not the day of the apostles. It is not the day of the prophets. It is the day of the saints. The Bible is clear that the Kingdom is inside every believer (see Luke 17:21). It doesn't say the Kingdom is only within Christian *leaders*. Too many Christians believe it is the responsibility of only their pastor to be the light of the world or it is for the people who are gifted or who have a personality that lends itself to shining. The Kingdom is power. It is inside you, and you need to take responsibility for letting *your* light shine.

A group of students from our youth group were moved to take personal responsibility to let their light shine on their school campus. They decided to fast lunch every day. They attended the Christian

Club meetings at lunchtime two days a week, and the other three days they walked around the campus praying and looking for people to minister to. Almost weekly, they came to me with another testimony of someone who had been healed or of someone with whom they were able to share the love of God. Faithfully they ministered to their campus. One day, in the middle of the cafeteria, they even laid hands on a boy who was blind. They didn't see him healed, but they were determined to let their light shine on their campus. Soon they gained such a reputation for prayer that even teachers began to approach them and give them prayer requests. They caught a vision for being light on their campus, took responsibility to do something about it, and saw that decision bear fruit. They didn't wait around for someone else to be the light of the world; they took personal responsibility to illuminate their own campus.

LIGHT WINS

Once you've taken personal responsibility to be the light of the world wherever you are, the next revelation you must have to shine effectively is this: *There is no competition between light and darkness.* Many people live with the assumption that there is some cosmic battle between light and darkness warring over their city, and it's always undecided as to who will win. Most of the time we aren't sure who is prevailing, or we believe darkness is overcoming. While there *is* a battle raging, it is not actually between light and darkness. Why? Because, in the words of Bill Johnson, "Light is always superior to darkness and darkness is always inferior to light."[1]

I love to read before I go to sleep at night. But I have never once headed upstairs to my room to snuggle up with a good book, turned on the light switch, and then waited as a battle warred between the light and dark. It's not that complicated; if I turn on the light, the darkness leaves. Darkness doesn't have an option. It doesn't hold voting rights. It doesn't stare at me defiantly and say, "I really like your room. I'm not leaving." Darkness doesn't have a choice, because the minute light comes into the room the shadows have to flee.

The University of California, Berkeley is considered by many to be the premier university for feeding anti-God and anti-religious philosophy into our culture. It is one of the darkest campuses in America. Erica Greve, the director of Campus Awakening, recently finished her Master's degree in Social Welfare at Berkeley. For one of her classes, she was assigned to write a report on a case study and give an oral presentation on her research to the class. She decided to be her own case study.

On the day of the oral presentation, Erica stood in front of her classmates prepared to tell her story. Many of them were professing witches, atheists, and homosexuals—not exactly a friendly environment to Christianity. She began:

> I grew up in a home where I was taught that religion was for the uneducated or for those who had no hope and needed a crutch to lean on. Religion was the "opiate of the masses." But then one day I encountered Jesus at a church. I knew immediately that God was supernatural and had a plan for my life. I was hungry to discover all I could about this supernatural God, so I ended up attending a ministry school in Redding, California, and while I was there I learned to do spiritual readings.

The class was absolutely riveted by this point, and the professor appeared to be somewhat stunned, uncertain of which direction Erica was heading with her report. She continued, "In fact, I would love to demonstrate what I learned at that school right now. Can I have a volunteer who would like a spiritual reading so I can demonstrate what I learned?"

Hands rose all over the room. Erica picked out a few and prophesied the good things God saw in them and the plans He had for them. She only had a limited time for her presentation, so as she was wrapping up she invited anyone who did not get a spiritual reading but wanted one to meet her after class. At the end of class, Erica made her way to the back of the classroom to find a line of people waiting for a word. For the next year she had people who had either seen her prophesy in class or heard about her from another person come up to her and ask her for counsel. They were inviting her to minister to them. Even in the darkest places, a little light causes darkness to flee.

When I go to a new city to minister, I often find that many people are unaware of this spiritual truth. Someone will pick me up from the airport, and as we are driving to our hotel they will begin to tell me how dark their city is. They inform me that their city is the capital city of witchcraft, or has more methamphetamine users per capita than any other city in the nation, or that the divorce rate there is higher than the national average, or that their city council is ungodly. They are trying to communicate to me how strong the darkness is in their city in order to explain why they are not experiencing revival. "Banning, you just don't understand. Our darkness is really dark. It's *dark* dark."

Come on, my revivalist friend. It doesn't matter what shade of darkness is in your city. That darkness will always remain inferior to even the smallest amount of light. Somehow we have bought into the lie that the enemy's darkness is stronger than our light or that sin is more powerful than grace. By being impressed with darkness we've come up with excuses for why our cities are not in revival.

HIDING THE LIGHT

This brings us to the next question we must ask: "If I am the light of the world and there is no competition between light and dark, why is there still darkness in my city?" Well, I'm glad you asked. The answer is in Matthew 5. For years when I read that passage, I was confused by Jesus' teaching about not putting a lamp under a basket. It seemed obvious. Why would Jesus instruct us not to do something that we obviously wouldn't do anyway? But then I realized Jesus was actually addressing the very plan of the enemy. It seems ridiculous in the illustration, but it is what most believers do—they conceal their light under a basket. They don't bring that light out so it can radiate to those around them. I mentioned before that, while there is no competition between light and darkness, there is a battle. It is fought over whether or not Christians will let their light shine. This is where the true battle is over a city.

Satan knows he can't defeat your light. He knows that when you show up and shine, he has to flee. So he works at convincing Christians to cloak or obscure their light. When they camouflage God's brilliance within them, the enemy can dwell in a region. It seems so simple, but it is true. If he can't defeat light he will persuade or induce the people who are the light to hide it. I see it again and again on campuses. In a school or college of 1,700 people, there are generally at least 200 Christian students—in other words, 200 people who Jesus says are the light of the world. Now that's plenty to radically impact a campus and see darkness displaced with light. It is heartbreaking to see that many campuses are completely untouched for Jesus, never influenced with Kingdom culture. The problem is that most Christians won't let their light shine when they are on the campus. They bring it out at church or among their Christian friends, but not in dark places. The enemy is not scared of Christians; he's scared of Christians *who let their light shine.*

One night during our weekly prayer meeting I kept hearing the Lord say, "It's time to go public." One of the things I've realized is that there is a major difference between my private life and my public life. For example, I have no problem singing at the top of my lungs when I'm listening to my favorite music in the car, the shower, or my living room. But prop me up in front of a crowd to sing along with one of my favorite songs? Not a chance! That's my private life, not my public life. And it's probably better for everyone that my secret ambition to be a rock star remains in my private life.

I'm also a private crier. It's true. I'm okay with admitting it: I cry. I don't know what it is, but I cry when I read books, watch movies, television shows, or commercials, or when I hear testimonies of healing. In fact, it was getting so embarrassing that I stopped reading certain biographies or stories of revival because I would start sobbing uncontrollably in the most awkward situations. I am a crier, but I am a private crier, not a public crier. There are certain things that were meant to stay in your private life. However, your Christianity was not one of them. Jesus never intended your light to stay in your private life. It was always designed to go public. To be released before others. To dazzle brightly with the luster of His heart.

Jesus told us, *"Let your light so shine before men…"* (see Matt. 5:16). Did you hear that? "Before men." Jesus said that we must make our light public. In order for our light to be effective it has to be exposed from beneath our covers and blaze before people.

One of the keys to the Welsh Revival was a revelation God showed Evan Roberts: "You must go public with your witness of Christ."[2] John G. Lake had the same revelation when he said you must have "continual public confession of what you are and what Jesus is to you."[3] This is where satan wages the biggest war. The devil covets our shine. He deeply fears the brightness of our rising. He desperately lusts for Christians to contain their light to themselves, and so he works overtime to make sure we do that. How?

We see the strategy of the enemy in the narrative of Shadrach, Meshach, and Abed-Nego in Daniel 3. It is one of my favorite stories because it describes how an entire nation can turn to God in a day. This is what I am pursuing, so the lessons in this popular Sunday school account have become extremely relevant for my life as a revivalist.

Shadrach, Meshach, and Abed-Nego were taken into captivity with the rest of the Israelites and brought to Babylon. There they were taught the customs, language, and laws of that pagan nation. They were foreigners away from home, just like Christians who are *in* the world but not *of* the world.

Daniel 3 records that the King of Babylon, Nebuchadnezzar, decided to build an image for everyone to bow down to and worship. He gathered all of the people together and declared that when they heard the music they were to bow to the golden image. The time came, the music played, and thousands of people bowed down to the image. Not only did the Chaldeans and Babylonians bow down to the image, the Israelites bowed as well. That is, except for three young men: Shadrach, Meshach, and Abed-Nego. In the midst of the thousands complying with the king's orders, these three revivalists refused to bow down. They rejected the directive to hide their light.

Now how did the king urge the Israelites, who understood the commands of God prohibiting the worship of any other god, to bow to his image? He used the same method satan administers today—peer pressure and fear. When you read the story, you find that the king invited a "who's who" list of impressive people—satraps, administrators, governors, magistrates, et cetera. The opinions of these leaders mattered immensely to the people of that day. The king knew that if he could convince that group to bow down, others would comply from sheer peer pressure. And if he couldn't get people to obey through coercion, then he would use fear—threatening to throw them into the fiery furnace.

His plan worked...almost. I hope you know how the story ends. Shadrach, Meshach, and Abed-Nego refused to be ruled by the king's menacing threats (the fear of people) or the fear of death. They ended up in the fiery furnace, but the Lord Himself showed up in the blaze and brought them out completely unscathed. The revelation of the power of God stunned King Nebuchadnezzar. The story concludes with him worshipping God and making a decree that no one could speak against Him, lest they be cut into pieces and their houses be made an ash heap. (See Daniel 3:29.)

Remember, the strategy of satan is to persuade you to hide your light because he knows the power of your shining. If he succeeds, then darkness will reign in your city, your workplace, your campus, or your neighborhood. Thousands of years later, not much has changed in how the enemy bullies, deceives, and restrains. Whether you're in school or have left school, peer pressure is still a real force. It doesn't just disappear when you finish your education. Most of us who are old enough to no longer be in school are still just as concerned about what other people think of us as we were in school; we just don't admit it anymore. As long as we are more concerned with what others think than with what God thinks, we will never go public with our light. Too many Christians run their lives according to others' opinions, and this prevents them from stepping out and embracing what God has called them to do. The reason is that the fear of people directly opposes faith in God. As long as that spirit is influencing our thoughts, we cannot hope to have God's perspective and priorities toward our circumstances. The fear of people neutralizes our impact on the world around us.

The sobering consequence of bowing to the fear of people is that we are actually keeping the people around us from opportunities to experience the power of God. The power that God has given us is not just for making us feel comforted or encouraged within a church meeting. Obviously we all need to experience the power of God for ourselves. But I believe that many of our encounters with the power of God are waiting for us at our schools, our homes, our jobs, and on the street—in the dark places. The light shines brightest in the dark. When we go public with our light like Shadrach, Meshach, and Abed-Nego, we actually create an opportunity for God to reveal Himself. We extend an invitation of faith that He cannot resist responding to. Like Chad's story, the most dramatic testimonies we will hear in the coming days will not result from church meetings. They will come from homes, the street, the marketplace, and schools as believers shine in dark places.

Scott Thompson, who is on staff with us at Jesus Culture and Bethel Church in Atlanta, told me a story from his days as a youth pastor in Fortuna, California. It is a great example of the impact you can have when you no longer care what others think about you. He halfheartedly challenged his students to stand on a bench at their school and shout out words of knowledge. They called him one day and testified they had done exactly that. Scott wrote me an e-mail to tell me about it:

> Three of them got words of knowledge—scoliosis, a stomach disorder, and an injured right ankle. They got

up on the table and yelled out to the students around them, "If any of you have these problems in your body, we need to talk to you." Within a few minutes three young people walked over. Each represented one of the words that were given. They said, "You wanted to talk to us." They told the students, "We are going to pray for you and you are going to get healed." They prayed for the girl with scoliosis and she got completely healed. She started bending down and pushing her hips forward. She said she'd never been able to do that without pain, and she was totally pain free. Next the girl with the stomach disorder—all the pain was completely gone. Last they prayed for the guy with the injured right ankle. He started moving it around and was completely healed.

These students created an opportunity for God to show up, and He couldn't resist meeting them there. He couldn't stay away from their faith.

HIS THOUGHTS

So how can we make sure that the fear of people doesn't negate our faith? I'd like to act as though it is easy to do and that I'm never concerned about what others think, but if I were to be honest with you I would have to say that it is *not* always simple, and I sometimes *do* care what others think. The only key I have found to shake off the weight of the fear of people is to remain secure in what the Lord thinks about me.

Did you know that God thinks about you? In fact, He thinks about you a lot. King David said:

> How precious also are Your thoughts to me, O God! How great is the sum of them! If I should count them, they would be more in number than the sand... (Psalm 139:17-18).

How did David know the precious thoughts the Lord had toward him? God told him about them. And God wants to share with you what He thinks about you, too.

This is why intimacy is so important. When I can abide with God and connect with His thoughts toward me, I position myself not to care about the evaluation or musings of others. The tension to be accepted is almost too much to bear unless you've encountered the thoughts of God toward you. You must position yourself every day to hear God's priceless considerations or reflections about you. His thoughts must override the scrutiny or deductions of anyone else. Then peer pressure loses its muscle in your life.

This new breed of revivalist will be a generation for whom peer pressure is powerless because they will have come to a place of security through their intimate encounters with Jesus. This is the reality behind Brandon Smith's ability to proudly tell his teammates that he is saving himself for his wife. Like Brandon, this new breed will know what He thinks about them because of their love for His Word and the things He speaks to them face to face. As they consistently experience His thoughts toward them the notions and attitudes of others will no longer control them.

Close friendship with God and a confidence in His Word are the driving forces for those who ignore fear and the allure of worldly persuasions and let their light shine. Not only that, I have also discovered that there is a direct correlation between your light glowing and your passion for the Lord growing. For years I have observed young people emerging to let their light shine and at the same time increasing their hunger for God. At first I couldn't figure it out, but then I realized what was happening. In the natural, if I light a candle only to put it under a jar, it begins to dim until it is extinguished and all that is left is smoke. The reason the flame of a candle dies out is a lack of oxygen. If you want the flame to intensify, you have to feed it oxygen. The more oxygen it receives, the more it increases in heat and size. In fact, fire can become so hot that if you try to douse it with water it just gets hotter. It's the same with the Christian life. Too many of us have learned to shroud our light under a basket without understanding that the flame requires oxygen. And *the flame of our hearts* needs God's breath regularly—more than just twice a week, when we bring it out at youth group and church.

HOW TO SHINE

If you are going to take cities you must embrace a life of personal responsibility to let your light shine, and you need to choose to live in the revelation that there is no competition between light and darkness. Finally, you have to answer the question, *"How* do I shine my light?"* We find an answer to this question in John 9. When the disciples asked Jesus whose sin caused the blind man to be born without sight, Jesus ignored their question. He simply said that His job was to work the works of the One who sent Him because He was the Light of the World for as long as He was here.

When He turned to the blind man and healed Him, Jesus was modeling what we are to do as the light of the world. When Jesus teaches us to let our light shine by allowing people to see our good works, He is not just talking about random acts of kindness. We've watered down much of Jesus' teaching on this subject by saying that He was encouraging us to be kind to others and meet their felt needs. Although He does teach us to do those things, He was saying something different in this story. That word "works" in John 9 is the same Greek word (*Ergon*) Jesus uses in Matthew 5. He is saying to let our light shine before people, that they may see things like blind eyes opening, the lame walking, the deaf hearing, the leper cleansed, and the dead raised. It's through raw demonstrations of power and radical displays of love that we let our light shine.

Paul, a high school student in Southern California, was profoundly impacted at our Jesus Culture Orange County conference and left the meetings on fire to display the goodness of God to people. On a regular basis he would stop and ask the Lord to show him someone in the room to whom He wanted him to speak about His love. Paul's friend was very impacted by the boldness of Paul but he was shy and afraid to step out. One day, Paul was in a restaurant with his friend and went about helping his friend learn to minister the love of God to others. He instructed his friend to pray and ask God, "Who do you want me to tell that You love them?" His friend prayed for a moment and said he believed God wanted to reveal His love to their waitress.

The waitress came over to take their order, but before she could do so Paul's ministry protégé turned to her and said, "Ma'am, we just wanted to let you know that God loves you." Instantly, the waitress threw down their menus and stormed off. A few moments later, she came back and slammed their basket of bread on the table.

"Who told you to tell me that?" She angrily demanded. "Who told you to tell me that?"

The boy, somewhat stunned by her response, said, "Ma'am, I'm so sorry. We did not mean to offend you. We were just praying and asked God who He wanted us to tell He loves, and He said you." Then the young man stood up and said, "And I feel like God wants to hug you. Is it all right if I hug you?" A bit shaky and beginning to cry, the waitress agreed to the hug. The young revivalist leaned forward and gave their waitress a hug right there in the restaurant. As he hugged her, she sobbed. He hugged her for a few minutes as she had an encounter with the love of God.

As she wiped the tears from her face she told them her story. "This morning I woke up and said, 'Nobody loves me. Nobody loves just me. God, if you're out there I need You to show me You love me.'" Because of the courage of these two young men to display their light, that waitress encountered the radical love of God and darkness fled in her life.

We've seen the power of this at work the last 13 years in Redding. Believers are living with a sense of responsibility to bring people into an encounter with a supernatural God who is passionately in love with them. Because of their boldness to let their light shine, darkness has been fleeing and glory has been released throughout our city. How has glory been released? It has been delivered through the promise of Jesus: As people see our good works, they glorify our Father in

Heaven (see Matt. 5:16). As we let our light shine by putting the works of God on display, slowly but surely we are seeing an entire city saturated in the glory of God. However, we know that there is a promise yet to be fulfilled, that *"the earth will be filled with the knowledge of the glory of the Lord, as the waters cover the sea"* (Hab. 2:14). The revelation of the glory of God will only cover the earth when the whole Body of Christ takes Jesus at His word and starts to go public.

CHAPTER 10

HISTORY MAKERS ARE RISK TAKERS

For years we have sent youth and young adults into the city to minister on the streets during our Jesus Culture conferences. And from very early on, we realized that it would be ineffective to teach people that they belonged to the new breed of revivalist without actually giving them a chance to experience it. In my years of working with young people, I've learned that sometimes they need a push—an impetus to take those initial steps of faith to discover they are revivalists. You need to motivate and encourage them to just get out there, receive a word of knowledge, and pray for people to have an encounter with God. It has been incredible to witness what the Lord has done through the lives of these young revivalists as they have moved out and taken risks.

Perhaps my favorite testimony of all happened at one of our Redding conferences. Scott Thompson, whom I mentioned earlier, was leading a group of young people to go out and minister in the city. As we do with all our teams, before they left the church he had them wait on the Holy Spirit to download words of knowledge. On this occasion, the word of knowledge they felt the Lord emphasizing came from a teenage girl. While she was waiting on the Holy Spirit she saw in her mind's eye a picture of a broken tree.

Their group was dropped off in a grocery store parking lot, but as they looked around for the tree they couldn't see anything similar to the girl's description. They decided to walk into a neighborhood to attempt to find the tree and unpack what God was showing them. As they strolled through the streets they saw a plumber standing by his van. The group approached him and asked if he needed prayer for anything. Immediately he blurted out, "Yes, my wife is an alcoholic." (As believers, we must realize how desperate people are in life, so much so that in this case a grown man would confide in a group of teenagers about his despondent situation at home.) They bowed their heads with him and prayed for his wife.

During this time, one of them received a word of knowledge about knee pain, so once they were finished praying for his wife they inquired if he had anything wrong with his knees. He looked at them in astonishment and asked, "How did you know I have knee problems?"

They quickly responded, "Sir, God speaks to us, and He told us you had knee problems." They asked if they could pray for his problem, knelt down, laid hands on his knees, and prayed for the power of God to be released. One of them prayed, "God, heal his knees. Take the water off of the knees and restore the cartilage."

The man stepped back, shocked. "How did you know I have water on my knees and how did you know I have missing cartilage?"

Again they said, "Sir, we already told you: God speaks to us." They asked if he would test it out. The plumber moved up and down and realized that all of the pain had left his knees. He had been healed.

The teenagers blessed him and then moved on to find the broken tree. One of the young people noticed a flyer hanging on a telephone pole which read something to this effect: "I am Jesus. I am looking for help. If you are an angel or can help me at all please call me." It included phone numbers along the bottom to tear off. One of the students with Scott suggested they call the number. Of course the entire group thought it was a great idea, so Scott reached for his cell phone and called the number on the flyer. After a few rings, a man answered the phone. "Hello," said Scott. "Sir, we found your flyer about Jesus needing help."

The voice on the other end said, "That's right. I am Jesus and I'm looking for help to accomplish my plans on the earth. But nobody is helping me. Every church I go to I get kicked out of."

He continued to explain his situation, and then Scott interrupted him. "Sir, you know how you can't go to sleep at night? You know how you just lay awake sweating and hearing voices that tell you that you are stupid and should kill yourself?"

There was silence for a moment on the other end of the line and then the man quietly said, "Yes."

"Would you like to be set free from that?" Scott offered.

"Yes, I would."

Scott proceeded to tell him it wasn't hard. He just needed to repeat a prayer. Scott started the prayer for the man to repeat: "Jesus..."

"Yes."

Scott stopped praying and explained to the man that he wasn't the real Jesus, and although he was created in the image of God the enemy had perverted that in order to make him believe he was Jesus. Scott then led him in a prayer of deliverance revealing to him the real Jesus. Scott heard a long sigh as the man said, "Wow, I've never felt this free and light." Scott then encouraged him to get plugged into a church and said good-bye. It had been a fun and exhilarating morning in the city already, but they still had not found the broken tree.

They walked a little further, and then the girl who had had the word of knowledge shouted out, "Look, there it is! Behind that gas station. That's the tree I saw." They knew God had something for them in the gas station convenience store. The group walked in and one of them asked, "Does anyone in here have a pain in their neck?"

There were two ladies working behind the counter. One of them sarcastically responded with, "The only pain in the neck around here is my boss," and walked off.

They approached the other woman and said, "Well that is not exactly what we meant. Do you have a pain in your neck?" She hesitantly admitted that she did. The group knew the Lord had brought them there to minister to her, so they asked, "Would you mind if we prayed for you?"

She pointed at a security camera in the corner and said, "I don't think my boss would like that. I would get in trouble."

Refusing to be turned down, Scott suggested, "Well, what if we act like we are buying a pack of gum? Slide your hand over to us and we will pray for you."

She agreed. And while they were praying for her one of them heard another word of knowledge regarding her family. "You have been experiencing relational strife in your family. You've been carrying this weight for your family recently, so much so that it is manifesting in a physical pain in your shoulders." The lady behind the counter began to weep. They ministered the love of Jesus to her and encouraged her in what God had for her family.

TAKING RISKS

That is just a normal day in the lives of this new breed of risk-taking revivalist. Everywhere they go, they are looking for chances to bring people into an encounter with God. As you can see, though, most of the time these opportunities lie on the other side of a risk they must embrace.

Randy Clark came to our church in 1999. It was the first time I was exposed to extended teachings on the subject of healing. I was gripped by what Randy preached and stirred to pursue a life of healing. I longed for the power of God to flow through me and bring healing to others.

My wife, SeaJay, and my friend, Lance Jacobs, were also passionate about walking in a healing anointing. We decided we had to get out and start praying for people to be healed in order to see healing released through our lives. Together we committed to going somewhere in the city every Thursday afternoon to look for people to pray for.

There was anticipation in our hearts the first Thursday as we all piled into my car and headed down to our mall. We had never done anything like this before but were excited to see what God was going to do through us. We arrived at the mall and started walking around, praying for God to release His healing power in our city and searching for people to pray for. It didn't take long to walk through the entire mall, so we found a bench in the center and sat down. We watched people wander by as we continued in our prayers for the healing power of God to be released in the mall and in our city. We had yet to pray for one person, but we were fervently interceding for God to show up and touch someone's life with healing.

About a minute after we sat down, people in need of healing started walking by. A man limped past on crutches. A lady with a cast on her arm strolled by on our right side, someone coughing on our left. But I sat there staring straight ahead, praying for God to come in healing power and hoping, "If I act like I don't see these people, maybe SeaJay and Lance won't notice either." It got so ridiculously obvious that the Lord was setting us up that at one point a gentleman in a wheelchair stopped just a few feet away from us. Still, we did nothing.

We silently got up and began to leave the mall, each of us knowing we were too scared to pray for anyone but not talking about it. Then, as we rounded the last corner before the exit, Lance turned to SeaJay and me and said, "This is not all right! We can't come down here to pray for the sick and not pray for anyone!" Both of us nodded in agreement but acknowledged that, though it was in our hearts to pray for the sick, we were scared. It was all so new to us. However, Lance refused to leave the mall without praying for someone, even if it was just for a headache to be healed.

As we were talking, Lance spotted a lady in a wheelchair. Like a missile locked onto its target, he headed straight for her. I was right behind him. I was scared out of my mind but right behind him. Lance struck up a conversation with the lady, who appeared to be in her fifties, and she told him her story. A few years earlier she had fallen off a ladder and broken her back. She had been in a wheelchair ever since. Lance, determined not to miss his moment, asked if he could pray for her. She agreed, somewhat reluctantly. Lance placed his hand on her shoulder and prayed a simple prayer of healing. It probably lasted no more than 30 seconds. Then Lance asked her how she felt. She said, "Wow! This is crazy. I feel a warmth all up and down my spine."

Thoughts raced through my mind, "Warmth! That's good. I think we are actually seeing someone get healed in the mall!"

Lance was feeling it now. Faith was rising in all of us. "Ma'am, would you mind trying to stand to test out your strength?"

What? I already thought Lance was crazy for actually coming over to pray for this lady, but now I was certain he was crazy. Then the lady, sensing that something was happening, stood up and said, "I haven't felt this strong in years."

At this, Lance was willing to lay it all on the line. He asked, "Why don't you try to take some steps?"

The woman looked at him, sat down, and said, "No, I would rather not do that." I couldn't believe it. She was so close. We kindly thanked her for allowing us to pray for her and walked away having learned a life-changing lesson: *History makers are risk takers, and radical obedience is the key to supernatural fruit.*

Lance, SeaJay, and I had an anointing residing within us to heal the sick, but as long as we stayed in our boat of safety and refused to take the risk of stepping out that anointing remained in the boat with us. I've seen this again and again—the anointing is released when you take a risk. The reason is that the anointing is released through *faith*, and faith always involves risk. As John Wimber said, "Faith is spelled R-I-S-K."[1] Peter learned this through firsthand experience:

> Immediately Jesus made His disciples get into the boat and go before Him to the other side, while He sent the multitudes away. And when He had sent the multitudes away, He went up on the mountain by Himself to pray. Now when

evening came, He was alone there. But the boat was now in the middle of the sea, tossed by the waves, for the wind was contrary. Now in the fourth watch of the night Jesus went to them, walking on the sea. And when the disciples saw Him walking on the sea, they were troubled, saying, "It is a ghost!" And they cried out for fear. But immediately Jesus spoke to them, saying, "Be of good cheer! It is I; do not be afraid." And Peter answered Him and said, "Lord, if it is You, command me to come to You on the water." So He said, "Come." And when Peter had come down out of the boat, he walked on the water to go to Jesus. But when he saw that the wind was boisterous, he was afraid; and beginning to sink he cried out, saying, "Lord, save me!" And immediately Jesus stretched out His hand and caught him, and said to him, "O you of little faith, why did you doubt?" And when they got into the boat, the wind ceased. Then those who were in the boat came and worshiped Him, saying, "Truly You are the Son of God" (Matthew 14:22-33).

Jesus wasn't just inviting Peter to walk on the water. He was inviting Peter into the realm Jesus lived in all the time—the realm of the supernatural. And He welcomes us to live there as well. Jesus is looking at us just like He looked at Peter and He is saying, "Come." He is inviting us to live a supernatural life. Can you hear Him calling *you?*

John G. Lake said, "Christianity is all supernatural, every bit of it."[2] We were born to live in the realm of the supernatural—the realm of healings, the prophetic, angelic encounters, and the gifts of the Spirit. It is the most *natural* thing for a Christian to live a *supernatural* lifestyle. Too many people are dissatisfied with their Christian walk because they are missing the element of the supernatural in and through their life. This new breed of revivalist who is emerging in the earth will be a generation that has embraced the realm of the supernatural.

NATURALLY SUPERNATURAL

When I was 19 I had a Beta named Oscar, which I loved. Betas are brightly colored fish with long, flowing fins. Oscar lived in a tank on top of my dresser, and every day I fed him a meal of tiny little worms. Oscar loved those worms. My wife, who I was dating at the time, didn't. SeaJay came up with a system so we didn't have to pick them up with our fingers. Her strategy was basically to hold the worms on a Q-tip and then drop them in Oscar's tank. Oscar, being such a smart fish, began to recognize the Q-tip and quickly associated it with dinnertime.

One evening I dropped the worm in the water, just as I did every time. But instead of going for the worm, Oscar lunged for the Q-tip. In that split second, I thought to myself, *Q-tips can't be good for fish,* and as fast as I could, I yanked it out of the water. But I was too late. I jerked the Q-tip up at the exact moment Oscar latched on to it, creating a catapult effect that launched Oscar across my bedroom.

I stood stunned for a moment, uncertain of what to do, then rushed over to where Oscar had landed. I clearly remember the sight of Oscar lying there on the carpet. It was truly pathetic. Oscar, once free and beautiful, was helpless, gasping for air. His fins were no longer flowing effortlessly as they had in the water but were pitifully draped across his body, unable to move. I carefully scooped him up and hurriedly plunged him back in the water. As he settled down into the environment where he belonged, he spat out a chunk of the Q-tip and was once again good to go.

I meet many Christians who have never fully embraced the life of the supernatural, and deep inside they know there is more to life than what they are currently experiencing. The reason is that, just like fish were created to live in water, we are made to live in the supernatural. John G. Lake describes it this way: "The spiritual realm places men where communion with God is a normal experience. Miracles are then his native breath."[3] The realm of the supernatural is where you will feel alive. It's where you will thrive. Miracles, signs and wonders, the prophetic, and supernatural experiences are where you were destined to live. But you can only inhabit that place by continually responding to Jesus' invitation to come out on the water.

DEMONSTRATING THE KINGDOM

First Corinthians says, *"For the kingdom of God is not in word but in power"* (1 Cor. 4:20). Therefore, if we are to be ambassadors of the Kingdom and proclaim its message, we must not only *talk* about the Kingdom but also *demonstrate* the power of the Kingdom. Jesus not only spoke about the Kingdom He was representing; He displayed it. We do the world a disservice by only honing our ability to communicate the Gospel clearly through words and not pursuing the anointing to demonstrate that Gospel through power.

Mark records a confrontation Jesus had with a group of scribes who believed He had blasphemed. They were offended because, when a paralytic man had been lowered down through the roof into a meeting He was having, Jesus had forgiven the crippled man's sins. The scribes believed that God alone could forgive iniquity and therefore interpreted Jesus' forgiving the man's sins as a claim to be the Son of God which, unless true, was heretical. Jesus responded, not with words, but with a manifestation of power:

> *But immediately, when Jesus perceived in His spirit that they reasoned thus within themselves, He said to them, "Why do you reason about these things in your hearts? Which is easier, to say to the paralytic, 'Your sins are forgiven you,' or to say, 'Arise, take up your bed and walk'? But that you may know that the Son of Man has power on earth to forgive sins"*—He said to the paralytic, *"I say to you, arise, take up your bed, and go to your house." Immediately he arose, took up the bed, and went out in the presence of them all, so that all were amazed and glorified God, saying, "We never saw **anything** like this!"* (Mark 2:8-12)

When Jesus' authority to forgive sins was challenged, He responded by healing the paralytic man. He didn't guide them through the Scriptures that clearly backed His claims to be the Son of God, although He could have. He simply demonstrated the power of God in their midst and let that be His answer. Incredible!

The world is still asking this question: "Does Jesus have the authority to forgive my sins?" Those in the world are drowning in their carnality and transgressions and suffering a sense of helplessness, unable to escape the pit they feel buried in. They want to know if the claims of Jesus are true. Can He set them free from the power of sin? We want to shout it with everything in us, "Yes, He does!" But it's not enough to say, "Yes." We must demonstrate that "Yes."

I'm not sure if you've ever had a salesman come to your home, but if you have you know they always arrive on the scene equipped with the product they are attempting to sell. Some of you might be wary of salesmen because you have been formerly convinced to buy a product that you either didn't need or that was of poor quality. However, successful salesmen close deals not because of their smooth talk but because they allow the product to speak for itself. I can argue with a salesman all day about the quality of a product, until I see it in action.

There was an *I Love Lucy* episode in which Lucy opened her front door to find an eager salesman ready to sell her a vacuum cleaner. He threw a handful of dirt on the floor and, grinning confidently, said something like, "If I can't completely pick up that dirt in two minutes and leave your carpet spotless, I will give you this $100 bill." Once the shock of the man throwing dirt on her floor wore off, Lucy was somewhat intrigued by the offer, so she agreed. The salesman whipped out his vacuum cleaner and demonstrated the superiority of his product. Sure enough, it did what he said it would do. The vacuum cleaner worked marvelously and left the floor spotless.

Imagine if the salesman had flung dirt on the floor but hadn't brought his vacuum cleaner to demonstrate how it could clean her carpet so quickly and efficiently. The conversation might have developed a little differently:

"What are you doing? Why did you just throw dirt on my carpet?"

"Well, I wanted to let you know that the vacuum cleaner I represent could clean up that dirt in two minutes without leaving a trace on your carpet."

"What! Where is your vacuum cleaner? Clean this up!"

"Well, I didn't actually bring my vacuum cleaner with me. But trust me, if I had brought it I would have blown your mind by how powerful this vacuum cleaner is. So, would you like to purchase one?"

"No! Go away."

It is somewhat of a silly illustration, but that is how many of us learned to evangelize—words with no power. We would highlight to people their sins and their problems and tell them Jesus is the answer to their situation, but we would never *demonstrate* that truth. This makes us ineffective in convincing people of that reality. As Dietrich Bonhoeffer said, "Truth devoid from experience must always dwell in the realm of doubt."[4]

We have to learn to expand the Kingdom of our Heavenly Father the way Jesus did. He always spoke the truth in radical love, backed by demonstrations of power, and those manifestations validated His authority and revealed who He was. For example, when John the Baptist became unsure whether Jesus was the Messiah or not, Jesus told John's disciples to go back and tell him what they saw—the blind seeing, the lame walking, and the deaf hearing (see Matt. 11:2-5). When people asked who He was, He pointed to the works He did. When the world asks us who we are, we should be able to direct them to what we do as evidence of the One we represent. Again, John G. Lake had one of the most profound revelations on the importance of demonstrating the Kingdom:

> Then you cannot only teach the theory of the atonement of our Lord and Savior Jesus Christ, but demonstrate its reality and power to save both soul and body...Men demand to be shown.[5]

THE KEY TO THE HARVEST

The Book of Acts says:

> *God anointed Jesus of Nazareth with the Holy Spirit and with power, who went about doing good and healing all who were oppressed by the devil, for God was with Him* (Acts 10:38).

This new breed of revivalist will be marked with an Acts 10:38 anointing—a baptism and enabling of the Holy Spirit and power—and I believe this anointing is the key to seeing what has been prophesied—the greatest harvest in the history of the earth. It will be brought in through demonstrations of power.

Acts chapters 3 and 4 make the connection between massive salvations and power. Acts 4:4 records that 5,000 men were saved after hearing Peter preach the Gospel. Now *that* is a good day in the Kingdom. But what was it that set the stage for 5,000 men to surrender their lives to Jesus?

The first section of Acts 3 tells of Peter and John encountering a man born lame. As was the custom of the day, the disabled man asked Peter and John for money. However, they didn't offer him the charity he was accustomed to. Instead, they turned to him and extended the greatest gift he had ever received: the currency of Heaven—the ability to walk. When Peter and John demonstrated the Kingdom *through power,* a crowd gathered. And when their audience heard the truth, they gave their lives to Jesus. The message of the Gospel, introduced upon a platform of demonstration, was evident, revealing God's heart for the broken and accompanied by a literal display of His power.

We are seeing this right now, not only in our own city but also in other regions, nations, and continents. Places like China, Africa, and the Middle East are seeing thousands upon thousands of people swept into the Kingdom, and they trace it directly back to God's power being released in their midst.

Jason Westerfield attended Bethel School of Supernatural Ministry in its early years. He is one of the most radical people I have ever met. His life inspires any who come across him to pursue the Lord with reckless abandon and to be a God-encounter to the world around them. One evening he was at a fast food restaurant in town and walked by a car with three guys inside—two were in the front seat and one in the back. Jason stopped and struck up a conversation with them. They told him that they were on their way to Washington. Jason then shared that he had just come from the evening service at Bethel and described what he had seen God do. I'm not sure how, but he ended up in the backseat of their car, sitting next to one of the guys, who was wearing a full leg brace. Jason told him about the love of Jesus and prayed with him to receive Jesus into his life.

Then Jason said, "You are a Christian now. You can pray for your leg to be healed and God will heal it. Let's do that right now." Jason laid his hands on the injured leg and invited the two guys in the front seat to do the same. Apparently they were up for it, so they laid hands on their friend as well. They released healing over the leg and then had the guy get out of the car to test it out. The young man removed his brace and began to jump up and down. The Lord had just healed him.

All of a sudden the driver turned to Jason and started confessing his sins. He concluded by saying, "I used to go to Sunday school as a kid, but I don't go to church anymore. I need to get right with God." Jason led him to the Lord right there on the spot. The third guy got saved as well. Then, as if that wasn't enough, they said, "Jason, we've got to be honest with you. We are in the middle of a drug run. We are taking drugs from Humboldt County up to Washington." They proceeded to pull their drugs out, throw them on the ground, and stomp all over them.

God is releasing the harvest through extreme encounters with power and signs and wonders. This new breed of revivalist emerging in the earth isn't going to just talk about the Kingdom but will also *demonstrate* the Kingdom. They are going to walk in an anointing of power that exhibits to the world around them that Jesus alone has the power to forgive sins.

GET BACK UP

If you are going to be someone who walks in the realm of the supernatural, you must first say *yes* to Jesus' invitation to get out of the boat. But there is one more hurdle you will face if you are to see power released through you. When Peter saw the waves swirling around him, the Bible says he became *"afraid"* (see Matt. 14:30). Fear will keep the anointing that is on your life in the boat. Fear of people and fear of failure are two things that will neutralize the power of God in your life. We often quote Second Timothy: *"God has not given us a spirit of fear, but of power and of love and of a sound mind"* (2 Tim. 1:7). Did you know that particular Scripture is written in the context of using our gifts for God? In the previous verse, Paul summons Timothy to stir up the gifts inside of him. When you desire to operate in your gifts it is sometimes scary. But the Bible proclaims that you don't have a spirit of fear; you have spirit of love, power, and a sound mind.

I talked earlier about the fear of people, but the other fear that despairs and debilitates us is the fear of failure. Bill Johnson told me one time that the difference between men and women of God who go down in the history books and those who don't is the former were not afraid to fail for God. We must progress beyond our fear of failure if we are to be effective in the Kingdom. So many of us are petrified of failure. We don't think we can cope with being confronted by our weaknesses and shortcomings. But the major problem with being afraid to fail is that you stop taking risks, and the truth about risks— the risks that flow from faith—is that they eventually pay off.

Peter failed. He began to sink. He walked for a while on water, but eventually the fear gripped him and he was submerged in defeat. But he never allowed the possibility of failure to stop him. You will face disappointment and deficiency as you step out and begin to take risks in the supernatural. You will lay hands on people, and they will not be healed. You will have a prophetic word or word of knowledge for someone that will be inaccurate. For all the testimonies of people being healed on the streets in our city, there are many stories of people *not* being healed. The point is we can't let our sinking blockade us from trying again.

There is no getting around it—you *will* fail when stepping out in the supernatural. It's what you do with that failure that really matters. Will it hinder you from ever stepping out again, or will you continue to press in? I really don't even like the word "failure" in this context. For example, if you step out in faith and obedience to pray for someone who is sick or prophesy over someone, then you are a success no matter what happens so long as you continue to learn from every experience.

There is a great story of Thomas Edison that illustrates this point beautifully:

> The genius inventor Thomas Edison was one day faced by two dejected assistants, who told him, "We've just completed our seven hundredth experiment and we still don't have an answer. We have failed." "No, my friends," said Edison, "you haven't failed. It's just that we know more about this subject than anyone else alive. And we're closer to finding the answer, because now we know seven hundred things not to do." Edison went on to tell his colleagues, "Don't call it a mistake. Call it an education."[6]

What a profound approach to life. If you wish to learn to walk in the realm of the supernatural, you must face your fear of failure and learn to embrace every situation as an opportunity to grow. Risks will eventually pay off. One day you will stretch out your hand to a man born lame and see him jump up healed.

One of the traps people become caught in when they are hungry to see the supernatural released through their life is thinking their risk has to be something gigantic. Most of the testimonies we hear are large and impressive in nature because they are the ones that seem easier to share. In fact, the majority of testimonies you read about in this book are not necessarily everyday accounts. I realize it is easy to hold back on taking a risk when you think it involves climbing into the backseat of someone's car, standing on a bench preaching, or some other act that is terrifying to you. Many of the risks you will take may not seem vast at all but are still crucial if you are going to release the Kingdom around you.

Kim, one of our former high school students, volunteered to accompany a girl who was not feeling well to see the school nurse. On their way, she asked the girl why she was ill. The girl told her she was diabetic and had not taken her shot that morning. Kim politely asked if she could pray for her. Unassumingly, as they walked to the nurse's office, she laid her hands on the girl's shoulder and prayed a prayer of healing for her. The next day the girl came running up to Kim with a huge smile on her face. "What's going on? Why are you smiling so big?" Kim asked.

"You remember when you prayed for me yesterday?"

Kim nodded, "Of course, on the way to the nurse's office."

"Well, I haven't taken a shot since you prayed for me and I feel fine!" By simply stepping out and taking what didn't seem like a big risk, Kim released the power of Jesus into the girl's life.

My wife and I prayed for a neighbor who had a staph infection in his foot and was unable to play in a hockey tournament that weekend. This young boy had already visited three doctors for the condition. He was on crutches with his wound wrapped in a bandage. In the middle of the street, we laid hands on his foot and released healing. The next day I looked out our window and saw him running around in his front yard with no crutches or bandage. I yelled across the street and asked him what had happened. He shouted back that he had gone to the doctor that morning and his foot was totally better. As he was racing off he excitedly told me he was going to be able to play in the tournament that weekend. Much of the breakthrough you will see occurs through simple acts of obedience as you step out and take risks.

While preaching at a church one Sunday morning, I saw a vision of a net in their sanctuary that was holding back water. I was confused at first because I didn't understand how a net full of holes could hold back water. I asked the Lord what it was I was seeing. He said, "That's a safety net. Safety nets can hold back what I want to pour out." Fellow revivalist, I encourage you to lose the safety net and don't be afraid to step out.

CHANGING THE WORLD

People with a vision to change the world are willing to take risks. The vulnerabilities that are required to live in the realm of the supernatural are risks we will take the more we are captured by the vision of Jesus. He is offering us the chance to change the world with Him. Something happens to us when we hang out with the most visionary risk-taker of all—Jesus. Acts says:

> Now as [the religious leaders] observed the confidence of Peter and John and understood that they were uneducated and untrained men, they were amazed, and [began] to recognize them as having been with Jesus (Acts 4:13 NASB).

The new breed of revivalist that the Lord is releasing across the earth walks in supernatural confidence and boldness because they have been with Jesus and abide in Him. They are His friends and follow after Him passionately. Risk-taking will be their signature. And these emerging faith-filled lovers of God will transform the world. It will be said of them the same that was declared about the early believers, "These who have turned the world upside down have come here too" (Acts 17:6).

THE CALL OF GOD

Years ago I read a story that struck me as prophetic for this generation. Again, I liked it so much I copied it down:

In 1983, John Sculley quit his post at Pepsi-Cola to become the president of Apple Computer. He took a big risk leaving his prestigious position with a well-established firm to join ranks with a small and unproven outfit that offered no guarantees—only the excitement of one man's transforming vision. Sculley says he made the risky move after Apple co-founder Steve Jobs goaded him with the question, "Do you want to spend the rest of your life selling sugared water to children, or do you want a chance to change the world?"[7]

Something inside us knows we were not meant to sell "sugared water" for the rest of our lives; we were meant to change the world. You and I will never be satisfied to just lead "good" lives; we were destined to make an impact. Our time on earth must change the course of world history. We long to see Jesus exalted in the nations and God's glory covering the earth. This is the call of God on our lives. We have been chosen to plunder hell and populate Heaven. God has entrusted us with the greatest revival the world has ever seen. Will you respond to God's call with every cell of your being? Will you give your life for revival? To see Heaven invading earth is why you are alive. This is why you were born. Seize the moment; say *yes* to Jesus with all of your heart. He will use you in ways you never dreamed possible as you partner with Jesus to see Him receive the nations of the earth as His inheritance.

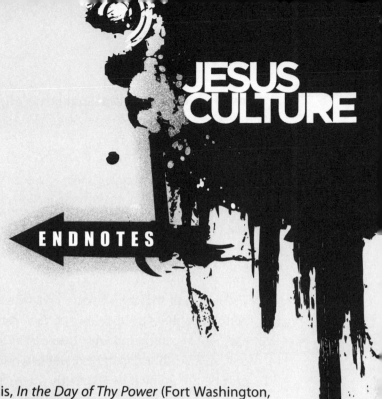

ENDNOTES

EPIGRAPH

1. Arthur Wallis, *In the Day of Thy Power* (Fort Washington, PA: Christian Literature Crusade, 1956), vii.

2. Wallis, In the Day of Thy Power, 20.

FOREWORD BY LOU ENGLE

1. Walter Wink, *Engaging the Powers* (Minneapolis, MN: Fortress Press, 1992), 285.

2. Bruce Wilkinson, *Dream Giver Course Workbook* (Sisters, OR: Multnomah Publishers, Inc, 2003), 6.

3. Wink, *Engaging the Powers*, 261.

CHAPTER ONE

1. From a sermon Wesley Campbell shared.

2. From a sermon Wesley Campbell shared.

3. From a sermon from Bobby Conner.

4. Winkie Pratney, *Revival* (Springdale, PA: Whitaker House, 1983), 143.

5. Wallis, *In the Day of Thy Power*, 51.

6. Winkie Pratney, *Revival*, 140.

7. Don Finto, "The Israel Time Table," e-mail, December 15, 2008. Don Finto, who has authored three books on the relationship of the Gentile church and the nation of Israel, emailed me this:

> The return of the Jewish nation was clearly predicted by the prophets by speaking of their return from the east, north, south and west (Isaiah 43:5-6), which can only refer to our day; by Ezekiel's famous dry bones prophecy in which he explicitly states that he [was] referencing the nation of Israel (Ezekiel 27:11); or by Jeremiah's forecast that [there would be] a future exodus of Jewish people back to their homeland that would eclipse their former return from Egypt (Jeremiah 16:14-15). Jesus' Mount of Olives discourse also foresaw a future destruction of the city (Luke 21:20), their exile to the nations, but their return (verse 24) as a precursor of His own return (verse 28). And Paul connected this return to the revival among the nations (Romans 11:12,15).
>
> Not as clearly predicted, but interesting in light of this fulfillment and the fact that there are no coincidences with God, is the parallel of the rise of Zionism (the first Zionist conference in Basel, Switzerland, in 1897) with the rise of Pentecostalism, the founding of the State of Israel and the healing revival in 1948, the return of Jerusalem to State of Israel in the Six Day War of 1967 and the beginning of the Jesus movement revival (*TIME* magazine's June 1971 issue three times points

to 1967 as the beginning of the Jesus movement), and even the release of the one million Russian Jews returning to Israel coming at the same time Russian communism fell in 1989. All of this lends credence to the faith that Israel is God's prophetic time-clock.

8.   Randy Bozarth, *The Voice of Healing* (Duncanville, TX: World Missions Advance, Inc., 2004), 71.

9.   David E. Harrell, *Oral Roberts: An American Life* (Bloomington, IN: Indiana University Press, 1985), 148.

10.   For more information, check out these two books: Roberts Liardon, *God's Generals* (Tulsa, OK: Albury, 1996), 311-346; and Owen Jorgenson, *Supernatural: The Life of William Branham* (Tucson, AZ: Tucson Tabernacle, 2002).

11.   For more information, check out this book and Website: Oral Roberts, *Expect a Miracle* (Nashville, TN: Thomas Nelson Publishers, 1995); Healing and Revival Press, "Oral Roberts," Healing and Revival, http://healingandrevival.com/BioORoberts.htm (accessed April 14, 2009).

12.   For more on Billy Graham, check out: "Billy Graham Historical Background," Wheaton College, http://www.wheaton.edu/bgc/archives/bio.html (accessed April 14, 2009).

13.   For more information about Kathryn Kuhlman, check out: Jamie Buckingham, *Daughter of Destiny* (South Plainfield, NJ: Bridge Publishing Inc., 1976), 104-15, 116.

14.   For more information, check out: David E. Harrell, *All Things Are Possible* (Bloomington, IN: Indiana University Press, 1975), 54.

15.   For more information, check out: "Healing Rooms," International Association of Healing Rooms, http://healingrooms.com/index.php?src=content&cid=3 (accessed April 14, 2009).

16. Liardon, *God's Generals,* 32-34.

17. Liardon, *God's Generals,* 34.

CHAPTER TWO

1. Aaron McMahon, *These Signs Shall Follow* (Aaron McMahon, 2008), 197-200.

2. Bill Johnson, "Here are those quotes," e-mail, May 12, 2009.

3. Transcript of Interview of Loren Cunningham on Original 7 Mountains Vision, "7 Spheres" (Nov. 19, 2007), http://www .reclaim7mountains.com/apps/articles/default.asp?articleid =40087&columnid=4347

4. This information is from a handout from Lance Wallnau at a Marketplace Transformation Conference at Bethel Church.

5. This information is from a handout from Lance Wallnau at a Marketplace Transformation Conference at Bethel Church.

6. Bill Johnson, "Here are those quotes," e-mail, May 12, 2009.

CHAPTER THREE

1. Sulu D. Kelley, "John Wesley's Notes on the Bible," Classic Bible Commentaries, Exodus 17, http://www.ewordtoday.com/ comments/exodus/wesley/exodus17.htm (accessed April 15, 2009).

CHAPTER FOUR

1. You can read his sermons in his book: John G. Lake, *John G. Lake: His Life, His Sermons, His Boldness of Faith* (Ft. Worth, TX: Kenneth Copeland Publications, 1994).

2. Harold Myra and Marshall Shelley, *The Leadership Secrets of Billy Graham* (Grand Rapids, MI: Zondervan House, 2005), 164.

CHAPTER FIVE

1. Bill Johnson, "Here are those quotes," e-mail, May 12, 2009.

2. This was in a sermon series I heard.

3. I heard him say this at TheCall San Francisco.

4. E.M. Bounds, *Power Through Prayer* (Springdale, PA: Whitaker House, 1982), 42.

5. Pratney, *Revival*, 175.

6. Andrew Murray, *With Christ in the School of Prayer* (New Kensington, PA: Whitaker House, 1981), 18-19.

CHAPTER SIX

1. Lake, *John G. Lake*, 62.

CHAPTER SEVEN

1. Frank Bartleman, *Another Wave of Revival* (New York: Whitaker House, 1982), 14.

2. Bartleman, *Another Wave of Revival*, 28.

3. Murray, *With Christ in the School of Prayer*, 44.

4. Bounds, *Power Through Prayer*, 13.

5. Murray, *With Christ in the School of Prayer*, 28.

6. Murray, *With Christ in the School of Prayer*, 25.

7. Wallis, *In the Day of Thy Power*, 85.

8. Bounds, *Power Through Prayer*, 44.

9. Bounds, *Power Through Prayer*, 45.

10. J.E. Orr, *The Flaming Tongue* (Chicago, IL: Moody Press, 1973), 15.

11. Solomon B. Shaw, *The Great Revival in Wales* (New York, NY: Christian Life Books, 2002), 76.

12. Warren W. Harkins, *I Saw the Welsh Revival* (Pensacola, FL: Christian Life Books, 2002), 31.

13. Buckingham, *Daughter of Destiny*, 146.

14. Buckingham, *Daughter of Destiny*, 147.

15. Bounds, *Power Through Prayer*, 29.

16. Buckingham, *Daughter of Destiny*, 147.

17. Bill Johnson, "Here are those quotes," e-mail, May 12, 2009.

18. "Shasta Dam, California," Bureau of Reclamation Homepage, Statistics, http://www.usbr.gov/dataweb/dams/ca10186.htm (accessed April 20, 2009).

19. Murray, *With Christ in the School of Prayer*, 10.

20. Murray, *With Christ in the School of Prayer*, 48.

21. Murray, *With Christ in the School of Prayer*, 31.

22. For more information visit: http://www.thecall.com/

23. Murray, *With Christ in the School of Prayer*, 39.

24. I have heard Bill Johnson many times tell the story about the missionary George Mueller.

CHAPTER EIGHT

1. Murray, *With Christ in the School of Prayer*, 46.

CHAPTER NINE

1. Bill Johnson, "Here are those quotes," e-mail, May 12, 2009.

2. Reimar Schultze, "What God Can Do," http://www.schultze.org/oldCTO286.HTML

3. Lake, *John G. Lake*, 389.

CHAPTER TEN

1. My friend Christy Wimber told me that her father-in-law, John Wimber, would always say, "Faith is spelled R-I-S-K."

2. Lake, *John G. Lake*, 451.

3. Lake, *John G. Lake*, 378.

4. Dietrich Bonhoeffer has been attributed with this statement.

5. Lake, *John G. Lake*, 164.

6. Ted Engstrom, "'Mistakes' Are Important," in *The Pursuit of Excellence* (Grand Rapids, MI: Zondervan Corporation, 1982), Chapter 3, http://www.cepnet.com/resources/ll/article.cfm?ID=111 (accessed April 20, 2009).

7.   WGBH Educational Foundation, "John Sculley," PBS, http://www.pbs.org/wgbh/pages/frontline/president/players/sculley.html (accessed December 13, 2007).

AUTHOR'S MINISTRY PAGE

For more information about Banning Liebscher
go to his website
www.JesusCulture.org
or visit his home church's website at
www.ibethel.org

BETHEL'S RECOMMENDED READING

A Life of Miracles
by Bill Johnson

Basic Training for the Prophetic Ministry
by Kris Vallotton

Basic Training for the Supernatural Ways of Royalty
by Kris Vallotton

Developing a Supernatural Lifestyle
by Kris Vallotton

Here Comes Heaven!
by Bill Johnson and Mike Seth

Loving Our Kids on Purpose
by Danny Silk

Purity: The New Moral Revolution
by Kris Vallotton

Release the Power of Jesus
by Bill Johnson

Secrets to Imitating God
by Bill Johnson

Strengthen Yourself in the Lord
by Bill Johnson

The Happy Intercessor
by Beni Johnson

Additional copies of this book and other
book titles from DESTINY IMAGE are
available at your local bookstore.

Call toll-free: 1-800-722-6774.

Send a request for a catalog to:

Destiny Image₍ᵣ₎ Publishers, Inc.
P.O. Box 310
Shippensburg, PA 17257-0310

*"Speaking to the Purposes of God for This
Generation and for the Generations to Come."*

For a complete list of our titles,
visit us at www.destinyimage.com.